PHILIP MASSINGER

Philip Massinger was born in Salisbury in 1583, the son of a retainer in the service of Henry Herbert, second Earl of Pembroke, whose family home was Wilton House on the outskirts of Salisbury. By May 1602, Massinger was a student at Oxford, though he never graduated, possibly leaving the university as a result of financial difficulties following his father's death. The first specific reference to Massinger as a writer is in 1613, when, aged thirty and imprisoned for debt with two other playwrights – Nathan Field and Robert Daborne – he wrote with them a begging letter to the theatre impresario, Philip Henslowe, asking for help to get out of prison. A description of him in 1620 by John Taylor, the water-poet, lists him as one of those writers 'which do in paper their true worth display', but Massinger may have been impatient for a box-office hit and keen to make it as a solo writer. Around 1621–2 Massinger's career appeared to take a new turn with the production of *The Maid of Honour*, probably his first solo play to be staged. In 1625, John Fletcher died in the great plague that struck London, and Massinger succeeded him as the King's Men's chief dramatist, for whom (with the sole exception of *The Great Duke of Florence*) he wrote all his subsequent plays at the rate of roughly one a year, including *A New Way to Pay Old Debts* (c. 1625), *The Roman Actor* (1626), and *The City Madam* (first performed at the Blackfriars Theatre in 1632, and first printed in 1658).

Massinger died in March 1640, aged fifty-six, and before the political tensions to which he had often alluded in his work finally exploded: the closure of the playhouses was less than two years away. John Aubrey wrote that 'he went to bed well, and died suddenly – but not of the plague'. During his career he wrote, alone or in collaboration, around fifty-five plays. Twenty-two are lost, and of the remainder, eighteen were written with other playwrights, fifteen alone.

Philip Massinger

THE CITY MADAM

NICK HERN BOOKS

London

www.nickhernbooks.co.uk

A Nick Hern Book

This edition of *The City Madam* first published in Great Britain in 2011 as a paperback original by Nick Hern Books Limited, 14 Larden Road, London W3 7ST, in association with the Royal Shakespeare Company

Originally published as a Globe Quartos edition by Nick Hern Books in 2005

Cover image: *John Bull and the Sinking Fund or A Pretty Scheme for Reducing Taxes and Paying off the National Debt*, published by Hannah Humphrey in 1807 (hand-coloured etching) by Gillray, James (1757–1815) © Courtesy of the Warden and Scholars of New College, Oxford/The Bridgeman Art Library

Cover design: Ned Hoste, 2H

Typeset by Nick Hern Books, London
Printed in Great Britain by CLE Print Ltd, St Ives, Cambridgeshire PE27 3LE

ISBN 978 1 84842 190 5

ABOUT THE ROYAL SHAKESPEARE COMPANY

The Royal Shakespeare Company at Stratford-upon-Avon was formed in 1960 and gained its Royal Charter in 1961. This year we celebrate 50 years as a home for Shakespeare's work, the wider classical repertoire and new plays.

The founding Artistic Director, Peter Hall, created an ensemble theatre company of young actors and writers. The Company was led by Hall, Peter Brook and Michel Saint-Denis. The founding principles were threefold: the Company would embrace the freedom and power of Shakespeare's work, train and develop young actors and directors, and crucially, experiment in new ways of making theatre. There was a new spirit amongst this post-war generation and they intended to open up Shakespeare's plays as never before.

The impact of Peter Hall's vision cannot be underplayed. In 1955 he had premiered Samuel Beckett's *Waiting for Godot* in London, and the result was like opening a window during a storm. The tumult of new ideas emerging across Europe in art, theatre and literature came flooding into British theatre. Hall channelled this new excitement into the setting up of the company in Stratford. Exciting breakthroughs took place in the rehearsal room and the studio day after day. The RSC became known for exhilarating performances of Shakespeare alongside new masterpieces such as *The Homecoming* and *Old Times* by Harold Pinter. It was a combination that thrilled audiences.

Peter Hall's rigour on classical text became legendary, but what is little known is that he applied everything he learned working on Beckett, and later on Harold Pinter, to his work on Shakespeare, and likewise he applied everything he learned from Shakespeare onto modern texts. This close and exacting relationship between writers from different eras became the fuel which powered the creativity of the RSC.

The search for new forms of writing and directing was led by Peter Brook. He pushed writers to experiment. "Just as Picasso set out to capture a larger slice of the truth by painting a face with several eyes and noses, Shakespeare, knowing that man is living his everyday life and at the same time is living intensely in the invisible world of his thoughts and feelings, developed a method through which we can see at one and the same time the look on a man's face and the vibrations of his brain."

A rich and varied range of writers flowed into the company and continue to do so. These include: Edward Albee, Howard Barker, Edward Bond, Howard Brenton, Marina Carr, Caryl Churchill, Martin Crimp, David Edgar, Peter Flannery, David Greig, Tony Harrison, Dennis Kelly, Martin McDonagh, Rona Munro, Anthony Neilson, Harold Pinter, Stephen Poliakoff, Adriano Shaplin, Wole Soyinka, Tom Stoppard, debbie tucker green, Timberlake Wertenbaker and Roy Williams.

The Company today is led by Michael Boyd, who is taking its founding ideals forward. His belief in ensemble theatre-making, internationalism, new work and active approaches to Shakespeare in the classroom has inspired the Company to landmark projects such as *The Complete Works Festival*, *Stand up for Shakespeare* and *The Histories Cycle*. He has overseen the four year transformation of our theatres, he has restored the full range of repertoire and in this birthday year we are proud to invite the world's theatre artists onto our brand new stages.

The RSC Ensemble is generously supported by THE GATSBY CHARITABLE FOUNDATION and THE KOVNER FOUNDATION

The RSC is grateful for the significant support of its principal funder, Arts Council England, without which our work would not be possible. Around 50 per cent of the RSC's income is self-generated from Box Office sales, sponsorship, donations, enterprise and partnerships with other organisations.

Supported by
**ARTS COUNCIL
ENGLAND**

NEW WORK AT THE RSC

We have between thirty and forty writers working on new plays for us at any one time and have recently re-launched the RSC Studio to provide the resources for writers, directors and actors to explore and develop new ideas for our stages. We also explore the canon for classics to revive and lost classics to re-discover.

We invite writers to spend time with us in our rehearsal rooms, with our actors and practitioners. Alongside developing their own plays, we invite them to contribute dramaturgically to both our main stage Shakespeare productions and our Young People's Shakespeare.

We believe that our writers help to establish a creative culture within the Company which both inspires new work and creates an ever more urgent sense of enquiry into the classics. The benefits work both ways. With our writers, our actors naturally learn the language of dramaturgical intervention and sharpen their interpretation of roles. Our writers benefit from re-discovering the stagecraft and theatre skills that have been lost over time. They regain the knack of writing roles for leading actors. They become hungry to use classical structures to power up their plays.

Our current International Writer-in-Residence, Tarell Alvin McCraney has been embedded with the company for two years. His post was funded by the CAPITAL Centre at the University of Warwick where he taught as part of his residency.

Re-discovered plays

The Swan Theatre was added to the Company 25 years ago in 1986. Over that time there have been many productions of re-discovered gems from the lost library of Jacobethan and Caroline plays which have gone on to earn their place in the modern repertoire. *The City Madam* by Philip Massinger is one such discovery.

The RSC Literary Department is generously supported by THE DRUE HEINZ TRUST.

This production of *The City Madam* was first performed by the
Royal Shakespeare Company in The Swan Theatre,
Stratford-upon-Avon, on 5th May 2011. The cast was as follows:

ANNE	**Lucy Briggs-Owen**
DINGEM/SERGEANT 3/ SERVING MAN	**Christopher Chilton**
LADY FRUGAL	**Sara Crowe**
MILLICENT/SECRET	**Liz Crowther**
OLD TRADEWELL/FORTUNE	**Kammy Darweish**
LORD LACY	**Nicholas Day**
HOLDFAST/SHERIFF	**Christopher Ettridge**
SIR JOHN FRUGAL	**Christopher Godwin**
SCUFFLE/PAGE/SERGEANT 1	**Michael Grady-Hall**
SIR MAURICE	**Alex Hassell**
MR. PLENTY	**Felix Hayes**
MARY	**Matti Houghton**
GOLDWIRE	**Nathaniel Martello-White**
HOIST/OLD GOLDWIRE	**Andrew Melville**
STARGAZE/MARSHAL	**Simeon Moore**
GETALL/SERVING MAN	**Harry Myers**
SHAVE'EM	**Pippa Nixon**
TRADEWELL	**Chiké Okonkwo**
RAMBLE/SERGEANT 2	**Oliver Rix**
PENURY	**Timothy Speyer**
LUKE FRUGAL	**Jo Stone-Fewings**

All other parts played by members of the company.

Directed by	**Dominic Hill**
Designed by	**Tom Piper**
Lighting Designed by	**Tim Mitchell**
Music and Sound by	**Dan Jones**
Movement by	**Struan Leslie**
Fights by	**Renny Krupinski**
Director of Puppetry	**Rachael Canning**
Magic Advisor	**Chris Harding** **Courtesy of the House of Magic**
Company Text and Voice work by	**Lyn Darnley**
Additional Company Movement by	**Kate Sagovsky**
Assistant Director	**Drew Mulligan**
Music Director	**John Woolf**
Casting by	**Hannah Miller** cᴅɢ
Production Manager	**Mark Graham**
Costume Supervisor	**Samantha Pickering**
Company Manager	**Jondon**
Stage Manager	**Janet Gautrey**
Deputy Stage Manager	**Francesca Finney**
Assistant Stage Manager	**Will Treasure**

This text may differ slightly from the play as performed.

JOIN US

Join us from £18 a year.

Join today and make a difference

The Royal Shakespeare Company is an ensemble. We perform all year round in our Stratford-upon-Avon home, as well as having regular seasons in London, and touring extensively within the UK and overseas for international residencies.

With a range of options from £18 to £10,000 per year, there are many ways to engage with the RSC.

Choose a level that suits you and enjoy a closer connection with us whilst also supporting our work on stage.

Find us online

Sign up for regular email updates at **www.rsc.org.uk/signup**

Join today

Annual RSC Full Membership costs just £40 (or £18 for Associate Membership) and provides you with regular updates on RSC news, advance information and priority booking.

Support us

A charitable donation from £100 a year can offer you the benefits of membership, whilst also allowing you the opportunity to deepen your relationship with the Company through special events, backstage tours and exclusive ticket booking services.

The options include Shakespeare's Circle (from £100), Patrons' Circle (Silver: £1,000, Gold: £5,000) and Artists' Circle (£10,000).

For more information visit **www.rsc.org.uk/joinus** or call the RSC Membership Office on 01789 403 440.

THE CITY MADAM

Philip Massinger

Edited by Cathy Shrank

DRAMATIS PERSONAE
Speaking parts in order of first appearance

Young GOLDWIRE Young TRADEWELL	}*apprentices to Sir John Frugal*
STARGAZE	*an astrologer*
LADY [FRUGAL]	[*wife to Sir John Frugal*]
ANNE MARY	}*her daughters*
MILLICENT	[*Lady Frugal's*] *woman*
LUKE [Frugal]	*brother to Sir John* [*Frugal*]
HOLDFAST	*steward* [*to Sir John Frugal*]
Sir [Maurice] LACY	[*a gentleman, suitor to Sir John Frugal's daughters*]
[PAGE]	[*servant of Sir Maurice Lacy*]
Master PLENTY	*a country gentleman*[*, suitor to Sir John Frugal's daughters*]
Sir John [FRUGAL]	*a merchant* [*and citizen of London*]
HOIST	*a decayed gentleman*[*, in debt to Sir John Frugal*]
PENURY FORTUNE	}*decayed merchants*[*, in debt to Sir John Frugal*]
LORD LACY	[*father to Sir Maurice Lacy*]
SECRET	*a bawd*
SHAVE'EM	*a wench*
SCUFFLE RAMBLE	}*two hectors*
DING'EM	*a pimp*
GETALL	*a box-keeper*
[SHERIFF, MARSHAL, three SERGEANTS]	
OLD GOLDWIRE	[*a gentleman, father to Young Goldwire*]
OLD TRADEWELL	[*a gentleman, father to Young Tradewell*]
[*Porters, servants, musicians, officers, Cerberus, Charon, Orpheus, Chorus*]	

Scene London.

Dedicatory Epistle

To the truly noble and virtuous
Lady Ann, Countess of Oxford.

Honoured Lady!

In that age when wit and learning were out-conquered by
injury and violence, this poem was the object of love and
commendations, it being composed by an infallible pen and
censured by an unerring auditory. In this epistle, I shall not
need to make an apology for plays in general by exhibiting
their antiquity and utility. In a word, they are mirrors or   10
glasses which none but deformed faces and fouler consciences
fear to look into. The encouragement I had to prefer this
dedication to your powerful protection proceeds from the
universal fame of the deceased author, who (although he
composed many) writ none amiss, and this may justly be
ranked amongst his best. I have redeemed it from the teeth
of time by committing of it to the press, but in more
imploring your patronage, I will not slander it with my praises;
it is commendation enough to call it Massinger's. If it may gain
your allowance and pardon, I am highly gratified, and desire   20
only to wear the happy title of,

Madam,

Your humblest servant,

Andrew Pennycuick

Act 1, Scene 1

Enter [Young] GOLDWIRE *and* [Young] TRADEWELL

Goldwire   The ship is safe in the Pool then?

Tradewell   And makes good
In her rich freight. The name she bears – the 'Speedwell' –
My master will find it, for on my certain knowledge,
For every hundred that he ventur'd in her,
She hath return'd him five.

Goldwire   And it comes timely,
For besides a payment on the nail for a manor
Late purchas'd by my master, his young daughters
Are ripe for marriage.

Tradewell   Who? Nan and Moll?

Goldwire   Mistress Anne and Mary, and with some addition,
Or 'tis more punishable in our house   10
Than *scandalum magnatum*.

Tradewell   'Tis great pity
Such a gentleman as my master – for that title
His being a citizen cannot take from him –
Hath no male heir to inherit his estate
And keep his name alive.

Goldwire   The want of one
Swells my young mistresses and their madam mother
With hopes above their birth and scale. Their dreams are
Of being made countesses, and they take state
As they were such already. When you went

	To the Indies, there was some shape and proportion 20
	Of a merchant's house in our family, but since
	My master, to gain precedence for my mistress
	Above some other elder merchants' wives, was knighted,
	'Tis grown a little court in bravery,
	Variety of fashions – and those rich ones.
	There are few great ladies going to a masque
	That do outshine ours in their everyday habits.

Tradewell   'Tis strange my master in his wisdom can
Give the reins to such exorbitancy.

Goldwire   He must,
Or there's no peace nor rest for him at home.   30
I grant his state will bear it, yet he's censur'd
For his indulgence, and for Sir John Frugal,
By some styl'd Sir John Prodigal.

Tradewell   Is his brother,
Master Luke Frugal, living?

Goldwire   Yes, the more
His misery, poor man.

Tradewell   Still in the Counter?

Goldwire   In a worser place. He was redeem'd from the hole
To live in our house in hell – since, his base usage
Consider'd, 'tis no better. My proud lady
Admits him to her table, marry ever
Beneath the salt, and there he sits the subject   40
Of her contempt and scorn and, dinner ended,
His courteous nieces find employment for him
Fitting an under-prentice or a footman,
And not an uncle.

Tradewell   I wonder, being a scholar

Well read and travell'd – the world yielding means
For men of such desert – he should endure it.

Enter STARGAZE, LADY [FRUGAL], ANNE, MARY,
MILLICENT, *in several postures, with looking glasses at their girdles*

Goldwire	He does with a strange patience, and to us
	The servants so familiar, nay, humble –
	I'll tell you, but I am cut off. [*Gesturing*] Look these
	Like a citizen's wife and daughters?

Tradewell   In their habits   50
They appear other things. But what are the motives
Of this strange preparation?

Goldwire   The young wagtails
Expect their suitors: the first, the son and heir
Of the Lord Lacy, who needs my master's money
As his daughter does his honour; the second, Master Plenty,
A rough-hewn gentleman, and newly come
To a great estate. And so all aids of art
In them's excusable.

Lady Frugal   [*to* STARGAZE]   You have done your parts here:
To your study, and be curious in the search
Of the nativities.   *Exit* STARGAZE

Tradewell   Methinks the mother –   60
As if she could renew her youth – in care,
Nay, curiosity to appear lovely
Comes not behind her daughters.

Goldwire   Keeps the first place,
And though the church-book speak her fifty, they
That say she can write thirty more offend her
Than if they tax'd her honesty. T'other day
A tenant of hers, instructed in her humour

	But one she never saw, being brought before her,
	For saying only, 'Good young mistress, help me
	To the speech of your lady mother', so far pleas'd her 70
	That he got his lease renew'd for't.

Tradewell   How she bristles!
Prithee, observe her.

Millicent   [*to* LADY FRUGAL]   As I hope to see
A country knight's son and heir walk bare before you
When you are a countess (as you may be one
When my master dies or leaves trading), and I, continuing
Your principal woman, take the upper hand
Of a squire's wife, though a justice (as I must
By the place you give me), you look now as young
As when you were married.

Lady Frugal   I think I bear my years well.

Millicent   Why should you talk of years? Time hath not plough'd
One furrow in your face, and were you not known   81
The mother of my young ladies, you might pass
For a virgin of fifteen.

Tradewell   Here's no gross flattery!
Will she swallow this?

Goldwire   You see she does, and glibly.

Millicent   You can never be old. Wear but a mask
Forty years hence and you will still seem young
In your other parts. What a waist is here! O, Venus!
That I had been born a king! And here is a hand
To be kiss'd ever (pardon my boldness, madam).
Then, for a leg and foot, you will be courted   90
When a great-grandmother.

Lady Frugal   These indeed, wench, are not

	So subject to decayings as the face.
	Their comeliness lasts longer.
Millicent	Ever, ever!
	Such a rare featur'd and proportion'd madam
	London could never boast of.
Lady Frugal	Where are my shoes?
Millicent	Those that your ladyship gave order
	Should be made of the Spanish perfum'd skins?
Lady Frugal	The same.
Millicent	I sent the prison-bird this morning for 'em,
	But he neglects his duty.
Anne	He is grown
	Exceeding careless.
Mary	And begins to murmur
	At our commands, and sometimes grumbles to us
	He is, forsooth, our uncle.
Lady Frugal	He is your slave,
	And as such use him.
Anne	Willingly, but he's grown
	Rebellious, madam.
Goldwire	Nay, like hen, like chicken.
Lady Frugal	I'll humble him.

Enter LUKE, *with shoes, garters and roses*

Goldwire	Here he comes, sweating all over;
	He shows like a walking frippery.
Lady Frugal	[*to* LUKE] Very good, sir.
	Were you drunk last night, that you could rise no sooner

100

| | With humble diligence to do what my daughters |
| | And woman did command you? |

Luke   Drunk, an't please you?

Lady Frugal   Drunk, I said, sirrah. Dar'st thou in a look   110
                Repine or grumble? Thou unthankful wretch,
                Did our charity redeem thee out of prison,
                Thy patrimony spent, ragged and lousy,
                When the sheriff's basket and his broken meat
                Were your festival exceedings, and is this
                So soon forgotten?

Luke   I confess I am
                Your creature, madam.

Lady Frugal   And good reason why
                You should continue so.

Anne   Who did new clothe you?

Mary   Admitted you to the dining room?

Millicent   Allowed you
                A fresh bed in the garret?

Lady Frugal   Or from whom   120
                Receiv'd you spending money?

Luke   I owe all this
                To your goodness, madam. For it you have my prayers,
                The beggar's satisfaction. All my studies
                (Forgetting what I was, but with all duty
                Rememb'ring what I am) are how to please you.
                And if in my long stay I have offended,
                I ask your pardon – though you may consider,
                            [*pointing in turn to the shoes, garters and roses*]
                Being forc'd to fetch these from the Old Exchange,

These from the Tower, and these from Westminster,
I could not come much sooner.

Goldwire   Here was a walk   130
To breathe a footman.

Anne   'Tis a curious fan.

Mary   These roses will show rare. Would 'twere in fashion
That the garters might be seen too.

Millicent   Many ladies
That know they have good legs wish the same with you:
Men that way have th' advantage.

Luke   [*aside to* GOLDWIRE]   I was with
The lady, and deliver'd her the satin
For her gown and velvet for her petticoat.
This night she vows she'll pay you.

Goldwire   How I am bound
To your favour, Master Luke.

Millicent   [*to* LADY FRUGAL]   As I live, you will
Perfume all rooms you walk in.

Lady Frugal   [*to* LUKE]   Get your fur: 140
You shall pull 'em on within.

Goldwire   That servile office
Her pride imposes on him.   *Exit* LUKE

Frugal   [*within*]   Goldwire! Tradewell!

Tradewell   My master calls. We come, sir!
           Exeunt GOLDWIRE, TRADEWELL

Enter HOLDFAST *with* PORTERS

Lady Frugal   What have you brought there?

Holdfast	The cream of the market, provision enough
	To serve a garrison. I weep to think on't.
	When my master got his wealth, his family fed
	On roots and livers and necks of beef on Sundays,
	But now I fear it will be spent in poultry.
	Butcher's meat will not go down.
Lady Frugal	Why, you rascal, is it at
	Your expense? What cooks have you provided? 150
Holdfast	The best of the city. They have wrought at my Lord Mayor's.
Anne	Fie on 'em! They smell of Fleet Lane and Pie Corner.
Mary	And think the happiness of man's life consists
	In a mighty shoulder of mutton.
Lady Frugal	[*to* HOLDFAST] I'll have none
	Shall touch what I shall eat, you grumbling cur,
	But Frenchmen and Italians. They wear satin
	And dish no meat but in silver.
Holdfast	You may want, though,
	A dish or two when the service ends.
Lady Frugal	Leave prating.
	I'll have my will. Do you as I command you. *Exeunt*

ACT 1, SCENE 2

Enter [Sir Maurice] LACY *and* PAGE

Lacy	You were with Plenty?
Page	Yes, sir.
Lacy	And what answer

Return'd the clown?

Page   Clown, sir! He is transform'd
And grown a gallant of the last edition –
More rich than gaudy in his habit, yet
The freedom and the bluntness of his language
Continues with him. When I told him that
You gave him caution, as he lov'd the peace
And safety of his life, he should forbear
To pass the merchant's threshold until you
Of his two daughters had made choice of her   10
Whom you design'd to honour as your wife,
He smil'd in scorn.

Lacy   In scorn?

Page   His words confirm'd it.
They were few, but to this purpose: 'Tell your master,
Though his lordship in reversion were now his,
It cannot awe me. I was born a freeman
And will not yield in the way of affection
Precedence to him. I will visit 'em,
Though he sat porter to deny my entrance.
When I meet him next, I'll say more to his face.
Deliver thou this.' Then gave me a piece   20
To help my memory, and so we parted.

Lacy   Where got he this spirit?

Page   At the academy of valour,
Newly erected for the institution
Of elder brothers, where they are taught the ways,
Though they refuse to seal for a duellist,
How to decline a challenge. He himself
Can best resolve you.

Enter PLENTY *and three* SERVINGMEN

Lacy   You, sir!

Plenty   What with me, sir?
How big you look! I will not loose a hat
To a hair's breadth. Move your beaver, I'll move mine,
Or if you desire to prove your sword, mine hangs   30
As near my right hand and will as soon out, though I keep
Not a fencer to breathe me. Walk into Moorfields:
I dare look on your Toledo. Do not show
A foolish valour in the streets to make
Work for shopkeepers and their clubs: 'tis scurvy,
And the women will laugh at us.

Lacy   You presume
On the protection of your hinds.

Plenty   I scorn it.
Though I keep men, I fight not with their fingers,
Nor make it my religion to follow
The gallants' fashion, to have my family   40
Consisting in a footman and a page,
And those two sometimes hungry. I can feed these,
And clothe 'em too, my gay sir.

Lacy   What a fine man
Hath your tailor made you!

Plenty   'Tis quite contrary:
I have made my tailor, for my clothes are paid for
As soon as put on, a sin your man of title
Is seldom guilty of, but heaven forgive it.
I have other faults too, very incident
To a plain gentleman. I eat my venison
With my neighbours in the country, and present not   50

My pheasants, partridges and grouse to the usurer,
Nor ever yet paid brokage to his scrivener.
I flatter not my mercer's wife, nor feast her
With the first cherries or peascods to prepare me
Credit with her husband when I come to London.
The wool of my sheep, or a score or two of fat oxen
In Smithfield, give me money for my expenses.
I can make my wife a jointure of such lands too
As are not encumber'd, no annuity
Or statute lying on 'em. This I can do,   60
An' it please your future honour, and why therefore
You should forbid my being a suitor with you,
My dullness apprehends not.

Page   This is bitter.

Lacy   I have heard you, sir, and in my patience shown
            Too much of the Stoics. But to parley further
            Or answer your gross jeers would write me coward.
            This only: thy great-grandfather was a butcher
            And his son a grazier, thy sire constable
            Of the hundred, and thou the first of your dunghill
            Created gentleman. Now you may come on, sir,   70
            You and your threshers.

Plenty   [to his SERVINGMEN]   Stir not on your lives.
            [Striking him] This is for the graziers; this for the butcher.

Lacy   So, sir.

                                                  They fight

Page   I'll not stand idle.
            [To Plenty's SERVINGMEN] Draw! My little rapier
            Against your bum-blades, I'll one by one dispatch you,
            Then house this instrument of death and horror.

Enter Sir John [FRUGAL], LUKE, [Young] GOLDWIRE,
                    [Young] TRADEWELL

Frugal   Beat down their weapons. My gate, ruffians' hall?
                What insolence is this?

Luke   Noble Sir Maurice,
                Worshipful Master Plenty –

Frugal   I blush for you,
                Men of your quality expose your fame
                To every vulgar censure! This at midnight   80
                After a drunken supper in a tavern
                (No civil man abroad to censure it)
                Had shown poor in you, but in the day and view
                Of all that pass by, monstrous.

Plenty   [*to* LACY]   Very well, sir,
                You look for this defence.

Lacy   [*to* PLENTY]   'Tis thy protection,
                But it will deceive thee.

Frugal   Hold! If you proceed thus
                I must make use of the next justice's power
                And leave persuasion and in plain terms tell you

Enter LADY [FRUGAL], ANNE, MARY *and* MILLICENT

                Neither your birth, Sir Maurice, nor your wealth
                Shall privilege this riot. See whom you have drawn   90
                To be spectators of it? Can you imagine
                It can stand with the credit of my daughters
                To be the argument of your swords? I'th' street, too?
                Nay, ere you do salute or I give way
                To any private conference, shake hands
                In sign of peace. He that draws back parts with
                My good opinion. [Sir Maurice LACY *and* PLENTY *shake hands*]

This is as it should be.
Make your approaches, and if their affection
Can sympathise with yours, they shall not come –
On my credit – beggars to you. I will hear   100
What you reply within.

Lacy   [*to* ANNE]   May I have the honour
To support you, lady?

Plenty   [*to* MARY]   I know not what's 'supporting',
But by this fair hand, glove and all, I love you.
                    Exeunt omnes praeter LUKE

                To [LUKE] *enter* HOIST, PENURY [*and*] FORTUNE

Luke   You are come with all advantage. I will help you
To the speech of my brother.

Fortune   Have you mov'd him for us?

Luke   With the best of my endeavours, and I hope
You'll find him tractable.

Penury   Heav'n grant he prove so.

Hoist   Howe'er, I'll speak my mind.

                Enter LORD LACY

Luke   Do so, Master Hoist.
Go in. I'll pay my duty to this lord,   109
And then I am wholly yours.
                [*Exeunt* HOIST, PENURY *and* FORTUNE]
                [*To* LORD LACY]   Heav'n bless your honour.

Lord Lacy   Your hand, Master Luke. The world's much chang'd with you
Within these few months. Then you were the gallant:
No meeting at the horse race, cocking, hunting,
Shooting or bowling at which Master Luke

	Was not a principal gamester and companion	
	For the nobility.	

Luke   I have paid dear
For those follies, my good lord, and 'tis but justice
That such as soar above their pitch and will not
Be warn'd by my example, should like me
Share in the miseries that wait upon't.   120
Your honour in your charity may do well
Not to upbraid me with those weaknesses
Too late repented.

Lord Lacy   I nor do nor will,
And you shall find I'll lend a helping hand
To raise your fortunes. How deals your brother with you?

Luke   Beyond my merit, I thank his goodness for't.
I am a free man, all my debts discharg'd,
Nor does one creditor undone by me
Curse my loose riots. I have meat and clothes,
Time to ask heaven for remission for what's past;   130
Cares of the world by me are laid aside.
My present poverty's a blessing to me,
And though I have been long, I dare not say
I ever liv'd till now.

Lord Lacy   You bear it well.
Yet as you wish I should receive for truth
What you deliver, with that truth acquaint me
With your brother's inclination. I have heard
In the acquisition of his wealth, he weighs not
Whose ruins he builds upon.

Luke   In that, report
Wrongs him, my lord. He is a citizen,   140
And would increase his heap and will not lose

What the law gives him. Such as are worldly wise
Pursue that track or they will ne'er wear scarlet.
But if your honour please to know his temper,
You are come opportunely. I can bring you
Where you unseen shall see and hear his carriage
Towards some poor men, whose making or undoing
Depend upon his pleasure.

Lord Lacy   To my wish:
I know no object that could more content me.   *Exeunt*

ACT 1, SCENE 3

A table, account book, standish, chair and stools set out

Enter Sir John [FRUGAL], HOIST, FORTUNE, PENURY
[*and* Young] GOLDWIRE

Frugal   What would you have me do? Reach me a chair.
                    [Young GOLDWIRE *fetches a chair*]
           When I lent my moneys, I appear'd an angel,
           But now I would call in mine own, a devil.

Hoist   Were you the devil's dam, you must stay till I have it,
           For, as I am a gentleman –

           Enter LUKE, *placing the* LORD LACY

Luke   [*to* LORD LACY]   There you may hear all.

Hoist   – I pawn'd you my land for the tenth part of the value.
           Now, 'cause I am a gamester and keep ordinaries
           And a livery punk or so and trade not with
           The money-mongers' wives, not one will be bound for me.
           'Tis a hard case. You must give me longer day   10

	Or I shall grow very angry.
Frugal	Fret, and spare not.

I know no obligation lies upon me
With my honey to feed drones. But to the purpose,
How much owes Penury?

Goldwire	Two hundred pounds,

His bond three times since forfeited.

Frugal	Is it sued?
Goldwire	Yes, sir, and execution out against him.
Frugal	For body and goods?
Goldwire	For both, sir.
Frugal	See it serv'd.
Penury	I am undone. My wife and family

Must starve for want of bread.

Frugal	More infidel thou,

In not providing better to support 'em.   20
What's Fortune's debt?

Goldwire	A thousand, sir.
Frugal	An estate

For a good man. You were the glorious trader,
Embrac'd all bargains, the main venturer
In every ship that launch'd forth; kept your wife
As a lady. She had her coach, her choice
Of summer houses, built with other men's moneys
Took up at interest – the certain road
To Ludgate in a citizen. Pray you, acquaint me:
How were my thousand pounds employ'd?

Fortune	Insult not

On my calamity, though being a debtor 30
And a slave to him that lends, I must endure it.
Yet hear me speak thus much in my defence:
Losses at sea (and those, sir, great and many),
By storms and tempests, not domestical riots
In soothing my wife's humour, or mine own,
Have brought me to this low ebb.

Frugal   Suppose this true,
What is't to me? I must and will have my money,
Or I'll protest you first and, that done, have
The statute made for bankrupts serv'd upon you.

Fortune   'Tis in your power, but not in mine to shun it. 40

Luke   [*to* FRUGAL] Not as a brother, sir, but with such duty
As I should use unto my father (since
Your charity is my parent), give me leave
To speak my thoughts.

Frugal   What would you say?

Luke   No word, sir,
I hope shall give offence, nor let it relish
Of flattery, though I proclaim aloud
I glory in the bravery of your mind,
To which your wealth's a servant. Not that riches
Is or should be contemn'd, it being a blessing
Deriv'd from heaven and by your industry 50
Pull'd down upon you. But in this, dear sir,
You have many equals. Such a man's possessions
Extend as far as yours; a second hath
His bags as full; a third in credit flies
As high in the popular voice: but the distinction
And noble difference by which you are
Divided from 'em is that you are styl'd

Gentle in your abundance, good in plenty,
And that you feel compassion in your bowels
Of others' miseries (I have found it, sir,   60
Heaven keep me thankful for't), while they are curs'd
As rigid and inexorable.

Frugal   I delight not
To hear this spoke to my face.

Luke   That shall not grieve you.

Your affability and mildness, cloth'd
In the garments of your debtors' breath,
Shall everywhere, though you strive to conceal it,
Be seen and wonder'd at, and in the act
With a prodigal hand rewarded. Whereas such
As are born only for themselves, and live so,
Though prosperous in worldly understandings,   70
Are but like beasts of rapine that, by odds
Of strength, usurp and tyrannize o'er others
Brought under their subjection.

Lord Lacy   A rare fellow!
I am strangely taken with him.

Luke   Can you think, sir,

In your unquestion'd wisdom, I beseech you,
The goods of this poor man sold at an outcry,
His wife turn'd out of doors, his children forc'd
To beg their bread, this gentleman's estate,
By wrong extorted, can advantage you?

Hoist   If it thrive with him, hang me, as it will damn him   80
If he be not converted.

Luke   [*to* HOIST]   You are too violent –
[*to* FRUGAL] Or that the ruin of this once brave merchant

(For such he was esteem'd, though now decay'd)
Will raise your reputation with good men?
But you may urge – pray you, pardon me, my zeal
Makes me thus bold and vehement – in this
You satisfy your anger and revenge
For being defeated. Suppose this, it will not
Repair your loss, and there was never yet
But shame and scandal in a victory   90
When the rebels unto reason – passions – fought it.
Then for revenge, by great souls it was ever
Contemn'd, though offer'd, entertain'd by none
But cowards – base and abject spirits, strangers
To moral honesty, and never yet
Acquainted with religion.

Lord Lacy   Our divines
Cannot speak more effectually.

Frugal   Shall I be
Talk'd out of my money?

Luke   No, sir, but entreated
To do yourself a benefit and preserve
What you possess entire.

Frugal   How, my good brother?   100

Luke   By making these your beadsmen. When they eat,
Their thanks, next heav'n, will be paid to your mercy.
When your ships are at sea, their prayers will swell
The sails with prosperous winds and guard 'em from
Tempests and pirates; keep your warehouses
From fire, or quench 'em with their tears.

Frugal   No more.

Luke   Write you a good man in the people's hearts

	And they follow you everywhere.
Frugal	If this could be –
Luke	It must, or our devotions are but words.
	I see a gentle promise in your eye. 110
	Make it a blessed act, and poor me, rich
	In being the instrument.
Frugal	You shall prevail.
	Give 'em longer day. But do you hear, no talk of't.
	Should this arrive at twelve on the Exchange,
	I shall be laugh'd at for my foolish pity,
	Which money-men hate deadly.
	[*To* PENURY, FORTUNE, HOIST] Take your own time,
	But see you break not. Carry 'em to the cellar,
	Drink a health, and thank your orator.
Penury	On our knees, sir.
Fortune	Honest Master Luke!
Hoist	I bless the Counter where
	You learn'd this rhetoric.
Luke	No more of that, friends. 120

Exeunt LUKE, HOIST, FORTUNE, PENURY [*and* GOLDWIRE]

Frugal	[*to* LORD LACY] My honourable lord.
Lord Lacy	I have seen and heard all –
	Excuse my manners – and wish heartily
	You were all of a piece. Your charity to your debtors
	I do commend, but where you should express
	Your piety to the height, I must boldly tell you,
	You show yourself an atheist.
Frugal	Make me know

My error, and for what I am thus censur'd,
And I will purge myself or else confess
A guilty cause.

Lord Lacy   It is your harsh demeanour
To your poor brother.

Frugal   Is that all?

Lord Lacy   'Tis more   130
Than can admit defence. You keep him as
A parasite to your table, subject to
The scorn of your proud wife, an underling
To his own nieces. And can I with mine honour
Mix my blood with his that is not sensible
Of his brother's miseries?

Frugal   Pray you, take me with you,
And let me yield my reasons why I am
No opener-handed to him. I was born
His elder brother, yet my father's fondness
To him, the younger, robb'd me of my birthright.   140
He had a fair estate, which his loose riots
Soon brought to nothing. Wants grew heavy on him
And, when laid up for debt, of all forsaken,
And in his own hopes lost, I did redeem him.

Lord Lacy   You could not do less.

Frugal   Was I bound to it, my lord?
What I possess I may with justice call
The harvest of my industry. Would you have me
Neglecting mine own family to give up
My estate to his disposure?

Lord Lacy   I would have you –
What's past forgot – to use him as a brother,   150

A brother of fair parts, of a clear soul,
Religious, good and honest.

Frugal   Outward gloss
Often deceives: may it not prove so in him.
And yet my long acquaintance with his nature
Renders me doubtful. But that shall not make
A breach between us. Let us in to dinner,
And what trust or employment you think fit
Shall be conferr'd upon him. If he prove
True gold in the touch, I'll be no mourner for it.   159

Lord Lacy   If counterfeit, I'll never trust my judgement.   *Exeunt*

ACT 2, SCENE 1

Enter LUKE, HOLDFAST, [Young] GOLDWIRE,
[*and* Young] TRADEWELL

Holdfast	The like was never seen.
Luke	Why in this rage, man?
Holdfast	Men may talk of country Christmases and court gluttony –

Their thirty-pound butter'd eggs, their pies of carps' tongues,
Their pheasants drench'd with ambergris, the carcasses
Of three fat wethers bruis'd for gravy to
Make sauce for a single peacock – yet their feasts
Were fasts compar'd with the city's.

Tradewell   What dear dainty
Was it thou murmur'st at?

Holdfast   Did you not observe it?
There were three sucking pigs serv'd up in a dish,
Took from the sow as soon as farrow'd,   10
A fortnight fed with dates and muscadine,
That stood my master in twenty marks a piece,
Besides the puddings in their bellies made
Of I know not what. I dare swear the cook that dress'd it
Was the devil disguis'd like a Dutchman.

Goldwire   Yet all this
Will not make you fat, fellow Holdfast.

Holdfast   I am rather
Starv'd to look on't. But here's the mischief: though
The dishes were rais'd one upon another –

As woodmongers do billets – for the first,
The second and third course, and most of the shops   20
Of the best confectioners in London ransack'd
To furnish out a banquet, yet my lady
Call'd me penurious rascal and cried out
There was nothing worth the eating.

Goldwire   You must have patience.
This is not done often.

Holdfast   'Tis not fit it should.
Three such dinners more would break an alderman
And make him give up his cloak. I am resolv'd
To have no hand in't. I'll make up my accounts,
And since my master longs to be undone,
The Great Fiend be his steward. I will pray   30
And bless myself from him.   *Exit* HOLDFAST

Goldwire   The wretch shows in this
An honest care.

Luke   Out on him! With the fortune
Of a slave, he has the mind of one. However
She bears me hard, I like my lady's humour
And my brother's suffrage to it. They are now
Busy on all hands: one side eager for
Large portions, the other arguing strictly
For jointures and security. But this,
Being above our scale, no way concerns us.
How dull you look! In the meantime, how intend you   40
To spend the hours?

Goldwire   We well know how we would,
But dare not serve our wills.

Tradewell   Being prentices,

We are bound to attendance.

Luke   Have you almost serv'd out
The term of your indentures, yet make conscience
By starts to use your liberty?
[*To* TRADEWELL]   Hast thou traded
In the other world, expos'd unto all dangers
To make thy master rich, yet dar'st not take
Some portion of the profit for thy pleasure?
[*To* GOLDWIRE] Or wilt thou, being keeper of the cash,
Like an ass that carries dainties, feed on thistles?   50
Are you gentlemen born, yet have no gallant tincture
Of gentry in you? You are no mechanics,
Nor serve some needy shopkeeper, who surveys
His everyday takings. You have in your keeping
A mass of wealth, from which you may take boldly
And no way be discover'd. He's no rich man
That knows all he possesses and leaves nothing
For his servants to make prey of. I blush for you,
Blush at your poverty of spirit – you,
The brave sparks of the city!

Goldwire   Master Luke,   60
I wonder you should urge this, having felt
What misery follows riot.

Tradewell   And the penance
You endur'd for't in the Counter.

Luke   You are fools.
The case is not the same. I spent mine own money,
And, my stock being small, no marvel 'twas soon wasted.
But you without the least doubt or suspicion,
If cautelous, may make bold with your master's.
As, for example, when his ships come home,

	And you take your receipts – as 'tis the fashion –
	For fifty bales of silk, you may write forty; 70
	Or so many pieces of cloth of bodkin,
	Tissue, gold, silver, velvets, satins, taffetas,
	A piece of each deducted from the gross
	Will never be miss'd: a dash of a pen will do it.

Tradewell   Aye, but our fathers' bonds, that lie in pawn
        For our honesties, must pay for't.

Luke   A mere bugbear
        Invented to fright children! As I live,
        Were I the master of my brother's fortunes,
        I should glory in such servants. Did'st thou know
        What ravishing lechery it is to enter   80
        An ordinary, *cap-a-pie* trimm'd like a gallant
        (For which in trunks conceal'd be ever furnish'd),
        The reverence, respect, the crouches, cringes,
        The musical chime of gold in your cramm'd pockets
        Commands from the attendants and poor porters?

Tradewell   Oh, rare!

Luke   Then, sitting at the table with
        The braveries of the kingdom, you shall hear
        Occurrents from all corners of the world,
        The plots, the counsels, the designs of princes,
        And freely censure 'em; the city wits   90
        Cried up, or decried, as their passions lead 'em,
        Judgement having naught to do there.

Tradewell   Admirable!

Luke   My lord no sooner shall rise out of his chair –
        The gaming lord, I mean – but you may boldly,
        By the privilege of a gamester, fill his room

(For in play you are all fellows); have your knife
As soon in the pheasant; drink your health as freely
And striking in a lucky hand or two,
Buy out your time.

Tradewell   This may be, but suppose
We should be known?

Luke   Have money and good clothes,
And you may pass invisible. Or if   101
You love a madam-punk, and your wide nostril
Be taken with the scent of cambric smocks
Wrought and perfum'd –

Goldwire   There, there, Master Luke,
There lies my road of happiness.

Luke   Enjoy it,
And pleasures stolen being sweetest, apprehend
The raptures of being hurried in a coach
To Brentford, Staines or Barnet.

Goldwire   'Tis enchanting:
I have prov'd it.

Luke   Hast thou?

Goldwire   Yes, in all these places,
I have had my several pagans billeted   110
For my own tooth, and after ten-pound suppers,
The curtains drawn, my fiddlers playing all night
'The shaking of the sheets', which I have danc'd
Again and again with my cockatrice. Master Luke,
You shall be of my counsel,
[*to* TRADEWELL]   and we two sworn brothers,
And therefore I'll be open. I am out now
Six hundred in the cash, yet if on a sudden

	I should be call'd to account, I have a trick	
	How to evade it and make up the sum.	

Tradewell   Is't possible?

Luke   You can instruct your tutor.   120
            How? How, good Tom?

Goldwire   Why, look you. We cash-keepers
            Hold correspondence, supply one another
            On all occasions. I can borrow for a week
            Two hundred pounds of one, as much of a second,
            A third lays down the rest, and when they want,
            As my master's moneys come in, I do repay it:
            Ka me, ka thee.

Luke   An excellent knot! 'Tis pity
            It e'er should be unloos'd: for me, it shall not.
            You are shown the way, friend Tradewell. You may make use on't,
            Or freeze in the warehouse and keep company   130
            With the cater Holdfast.

Tradewell   No, I am converted.
            A Barbican broker will furnish me with outside,
            And then, a crash at the ordinary.

Goldwire   [to LUKE]   I am for
            The lady you saw this morning, who indeed is
            My proper recreation.

Luke   Go to, Tom!
            What did you make me?

Goldwire   I'll do as much for you:
            Employ me when you please.

Luke   If you are inquir'd for,
            I will excuse you both.

Tradewell	Kind master Luke!
Goldwire	We'll break my master to make you, you know. 139
Luke	I cannot love money. Go, boys. [*Aside*] When time serves,
	It shall appear. I have another end in't. *Exeunt*

[ACT 2, SCENE 2]

A chair set out

Enter LORD Lacy, Sir John [FRUGAL], [Sir Maurice] LACY,
PLENTY, LADY [FRUGAL], ANNE, MARY [*and*] MILLICENT

Frugal   Ten thousand pounds apiece I'll make their portions,
And after my decease, it shall be double,
Provided you assure them for their jointures
Eight hundred pounds *per annum*, and entail
A thousand more upon the heirs male
Begotten on their bodies.

Lord Lacy   Sir, you bind us
To very strict conditions.

Plenty   You, my lord,
May do as you please, but to me it seems strange
We should conclude of portions and of jointures
Before our hearts are settled.

Lady Frugal   You say right. [*She sits*]   10
There are counsels of more moment and importance
On the making up of marriages to be
Consider'd duly than the portion or the jointures
In which a mother's care must be exacted,

	And I by special privilege may challenge	
	A casting voice.	
Lord Lacy	How's this?	
Lady Frugal	Even so, my lord,	
	In these affairs I govern.	
Lord Lacy	[*to* FRUGAL] Give you way to't?	
Frugal	I must, my lord.	
Lady Frugal	'Tis fit he should and shall.	
	You may consult of something else; this province	
	Is wholly mine.	
Lacy	By the city custom, madam?	20
Lady Frugal	Yes, my young sir, and both must look my daughters	
	Will hold it by my copy.	
Plenty	Brave, i' faith!	
Frugal	Give her leave to talk; we have the power to do.	
	[*To* LORD LACY] And now, touching the business we last	
	talk'd of.	
	In private, if you please.	
Lord Lacy	[*to* FRUGAL] 'Tis well remember'd –	
	[*to* LADY FRUGAL] You shall take your own way, madam.	

Exeunt LORD LACY *and* FRUGAL

Lacy	What strange lecture	
	Will she read unto us?	
Lady Frugal	Such as wisdom warrants	
	From the superior bodies. Is Stargaze ready	
	With his several schemes?	
Millicent	Yes, madam, and attends	

Your pleasure.

Lacy	Stargaze, lady? What is he? 30
Lady Frugal	Call him in. *Exit* MILLICENT

You shall first know him, then admire him
For a man of many parts, and those parts, rare ones.
He's everything, indeed: parcel physician,
And as such, prescribes my diet and foretells
My dreams when I eat potatoes; parcel poet,
And sings encomiums to my virtues sweetly;
My antecedent, or my gentleman usher,
And as the stars move, with that due proportion
He walks before me; but an absolute master
In the calculation of nativities,   40
Guided by that ne'er-erring science call'd
Judicial astrology.

Plenty   Stargaze! Sure,
I have a penny almanac about me,
Inscrib'd to you, as to his patroness,
In his name publish'd.

Lady Frugal   Keep it as a jewel.
Some statesmen that I will not name are wholly
Govern'd by his predictions, for they serve
For any latitude in Christendom,
As well as our own climate.

Enter MILLICENT *and* STARGAZE *with two schemes*

Lacy   I believe so.

Plenty   Must we couple by the almanac?

Lady Frugal   Be silent,   50
[*to* STARGAZE] And e'er we do articulate – much more
Grow to a full conclusion – instruct us

Whether this day and hour, by the planets, promise
Happy success in marriage.

Stargaze   *In omni*
               Parte et toto.

Plenty   Good learn'd sir, in English,
               And since it is resolv'd we must be coxcombs,
               Make us so in our own language.

Stargaze   You are pleasant.
               Thus, in our vulgar tongue, then.

Lady Frugal   Pray you, observe him.

Stargaze   Venus in the west angle, the house of marriage, the
               seventh house, in trine of Mars, in conjunction of   60
               Luna, and Mars almuten, or lord of the horoscope –

Plenty   Hoyday!

Lady Frugal   The angel's language! I am ravish'd! Forward!

Stargaze   Mars (as I said), lord of the horoscope or geniture, in
               mutual reception of each other – she in her exaltation,
               and he in his triplicity trine and face – assure a fortunate
               combination to Hymen, excellent prosperous and
               happy.

Lady Frugal Kneel, and give thanks.   [ANNE *and* MARY *kneel*]

Lacy   For what we understand not.

Plenty   And have as little faith in't.

Lady Frugal   Be credulous.
               To me, 'tis oracle.

Stargaze   Now for the sov'reignty   70
               Of my future ladies, your daughters, after

They are married.

Plenty	Wearing the breeches, you mean.

Lady Frugal   Touch that point home: it is a principal one, and
With London ladies, of main consideration.

Stargaze   This is infallible: Saturn out of all dignities in his
detriment and fall, combust; and Venus in the south
angle elevated above him (lady of both their nativities),
in her essential and accidental dignities, occidental
from the sun, oriental from the angle of the east, in   79
cazimi of the sun, in her joy, and free from the malevolent
beams of infortunes; in a sign commanding and Mars
in a constellation obeying; she fortunate and he dejected,
the disposers of marriage in the radix of the native in
feminine figures, argue, foretell and declare rule, pre-
eminence and absolute sovereignty in women.

Lacy   Is't possible?

Stargaze   'Tis drawn, I assure you, from the aphorisms of the
old Chaldeans, Zoroastes (the first and greatest magician),
Mercurius Trismegistus, the later Ptolemy, and the
everlasting prognosticator, old Erra Pater.   90

Lady Frugal   Are you yet satisfied?

Plenty   In what?

Lady Frugal   That you
Are bound to obey your wives, it being so
Determin'd by the stars, against whose influence
There is no opposition.

Plenty   Since I must
Be married by the almanac, as I may be,

           'Twere requisite the services and duties,
           Which (as you say) I must pay to my wife,
           Were set down in the calendar.

Lacy   With the date
           Of my apprenticeship.

Lady Frugal   [*to* ANNE *and* MARY] Make your demands.
           [*To the suitors*] I'll sit as moderatrix, if they press you   100
           With over-hard conditions.

Lacy   Mine hath the van.
           [*To* ANNE] I stand your charge, sweet.

Stargaze   Silence.

Anne   I require first
           (And that since 'tis in fashion with kind husbands,
           In civil manners you must grant) my will
           In all things whatsoever and that will
           To be obey'd, not argued.

Lady Frugal   And good reason.

Plenty   A gentle *imprimis*!

Lacy   This in gross contains all.
           But your special items, lady?

Anne   When I am one
           (And you are honour'd to be styl'd my husband)
           To urge my having my page, my gentleman-usher,   110
           My woman sworn to my secrets, my caroche
           Drawn by six Flanders mares, my coachman, grooms
           Postilion and footmen.

Lacy   Is there ought else
           To be demanded?

Anne	Yes, sir: mine own doctor;
	French and Italian cooks, musicians, songsters,
	And a chaplain that must preach to please my fancy;
	A friend at court to place me at a masque;
	The private box took up at a new play
	For me and my retinue; a fresh habit
	(Of a fashion never seen before) to draw 120
	The gallants' eyes that sit on the stage upon me;
	Some decay'd lady for my parasite
	To flatter me and rail at other madams.
	And there ends my ambition.
Lacy	[*sarcastically*] Your desires
	Are modest, I confess.
Anne	These toys subscrib'd to,
	And you continuing an obedient husband
	Upon all fit occasions, you shall find me
	A most indulgent wife.
Lady Frugal	You have said. Give place
	And hear your younger sister.
Plenty	[*aside to* LACY] If she speak 129
	Her language, may the Great Fiend booted and spurr'd,
	With a scythe at his girdle (as the Scotchman says),
	Ride headlong down her throat.
Lacy	[*aside to* PLENTY] Curse not the judge
	Before you hear the sentence.
Mary	In some part
	My sister hath spoke well for the city pleasures,
	But I am for the country's, and must say,
	Under correction, in her demands
	She was too modest.

Lacy	[*aside to* PLENTY] How like you this exordium?
Plenty	[*aside to* LACY] Too modest, with a mischief!
Mary	[*overhearing him*] Yes, too modest.
	I know my value and prize it to the worth:
	My youth, my beauty –
Plenty	[*aside*] How your glass deceives you! 140
Mary	– The greatness of the portion I bring with me,
	And the sea of happiness that from me flows to you.
Lacy	She bears up close.
Mary	And can you in your wisdom,
	Or rustical simplicity, imagine
	You have met some innocent country girl, that never
	Look'd further than her father's farm, nor knew more
	Than the price of corn in the market, or at what rate
	Beef went a stone? That would survey your dairy
	And bring in mutton out of cheese and butter?
	That could give directions at what time of the moon 150
	To cut her cocks for capons against Christmas,
	Or when to raise up goslings?
Plenty	These are arts
	Would not misbecome you, though you should put in
	Obedience and duty.
Mary	Yes, and patience
	To sit like a fool at home and eye your threshers,
	Then make provision for your slavering hounds
	When you come drunk from an alehouse after hunting
	With your clowns and comrades as if all were yours,
	You the lord paramount, and I the drudge.
	The case, sir, must be otherwise.

Plenty	How, I beseech you?

Mary Marry, thus: I will not, like my sister, challenge   161
What's useful or superfluous from my husband.
That's base all o'er. Mine shall receive from me
What I think fit. I'll have the state convey'd
Into my hands, and he put to his pension,
Which the wise viragos of our climate practise.
I will receive your rents –

Plenty   You shall be hang'd first.

Mary – Make sale or purchase. Nay, I'll have my neighbours
Instructed, when a passenger shall ask,
'Whose house is this?' – though you stand by – to answer,
'The Lady Plenty's'. Or 'Who owes this manor?'   171
'The Lady Plenty.' 'Whose sheep are these? Whose oxen?'
'The Lady Plenty's.'

Plenty   A plentiful pox upon you.

Mary And when I have children, if it be inquir'd
By a stranger whose they are, they shall still echo
'My Lady Plenty's', the husband never thought on.

Plenty In their begetting, I think so.

Mary   Since you'll marry
In the city for our wealth, in justice, we
Must have the country's sovereignty.

Plenty   And we, nothing.

Mary A nag of forty shillings, a couple of spaniels   180
With a sparhawk is sufficient, and these too,
As you shall behave yourself, during my pleasure,
I will not greatly stand on. I have said, sir.
Now, if you like me, so.

Lady Frugal	At my entreaty,
	The articles shall be easier.
Plenty	Shall they, i'faith?
	Like bitch, like whelps.
Lacy	Use fair words.
Plenty	I cannot.
	I have read of a House of Pride, and now I have found one:
	A whirlwind overturn it!
Lacy	[*to* ANNE] On these terms,
	Will your minxship be a lady?
Plenty	A lady in a morris.
	I'll wed a pedlar's punk first.
Lacy	Tinker's trull, 190
	A beggar without a smock.
Plenty	[*to* MARY] Let Monsieur Almanac,
	Since he is so cunning with his Jacob's staff,
	Find you out a husband in a bowling alley.
Lacy	The general pimp to a brothel.
Plenty	[*to* MARY] Though that now
	All the loose desires of man were rak'd up in me,
	And no means but thy maidenhead left to quench 'em,
	I would turn cinders, or the next sow-gelder
	– On my life – should lib me, rather than embrace thee.
Anne	Wooing do you call this?
Mary	A bear-baiting, rather.
Plenty	Were you worried, you deserve it, and I hope 200
	I shall live to see it.
Lacy	I'll not rail, nor curse you.

	Only this: you are pretty peats, and your great portions
	Adds much unto your handsomeness, but as
	You would command your husbands, you are beggars,
	Deform'd and ugly.

Lady Frugal   Hear me.

Plenty   Not a word more.
                    Exeunt [Sir Maurice] LACY *and* PLENTY

Anne   [*weeping*] I ever thought 'twould come to this.

Mary   [*weeping, to* STARGAZE]   We may
            Lead apes in hell for husbands, if you bind us
            T'articulate thus with our suitors.

Stargaze   Now the cloud breaks,
            And the storm will fall on me.

Lady Frugal   [*to* STARGAZE]   You rascal, juggler!
                    She breaks his head and beats him

Stargaze   Dear madam –

Lady Frugal   Hold you intelligence with the stars   210
            And thus deceive me?

Stargaze   My art cannot err.
            If it does, I'll burn my astrolabe. In mine own star,
            I did foresee this broken head and beating,
            And now your ladyship sees, as I do feel it,
            It could not be avoided.

Lady Frugal   Did you?

Stargaze   Madam,
            Have patience but a week, and if you find not
            All my predictions true touching your daughters,
            And a change of fortune to yourself (a rare one),

Turn me out of doors. These are not the men the planets
Appointed for their husbands. There will come   220
Gallants of another mettle.

Millicent   Once more trust him.

Anne & Mary Do, lady mother.

Lady Frugal [*to* STARGAZE]   I am vex'd. Look to it.
Turn o'er your books. If once again you fool me,
You shall graze elsewhere. Come, girls.
                    Exeunt [*all except* STARGAZE]

Stargaze   I am glad I scap'd thus.
                                        [*Exit*]

ACT 2, SCENE 3

Enter LORD [LACY] *and* Sir John [FRUGAL]

Lord Lacy The plot shows very likely.

Frugal   I repose
My principal trust in your lordship; 'twill prepare
The physic I intend to minister
To my wife and daughters.

Lord Lacy   I will do my parts
To set it off to the life.

              Enter [Sir Maurice] LACY *and* PLENTY

Frugal   It may produce
A scene of no vulgar mirth. Here come the suitors.
When we understand how they relish my wife's humours,
The rest is feasible.

Lord Lacy	Their looks are cloudy.
Frugal	How sits the wind? Are you ready to launch forth Into this sea of marriage?
Plenty	Call it rather 10 A whirlpool of afflictions.
Lacy	If you please To enjoin me to it, I will undertake To find the north passage to the Indies sooner Than plough with your proud heifer.
Plenty	I will make A voyage to hell first –
Frugal	How, sir!
Plenty	– And court Proserpine In the sight of Pluto, his three-headed porter Cerberus standing by and all the furies, With their whips to scourge me for't, than say, 'I, Jeffrey, Take your Mary for my wife'.
Lord Lacy	Why, what's the matter?
Lacy	The matter is, the mother (with your pardon, 20 I cannot but speak so much) is a most insufferable, Proud, insolent lady.
Plenty	And the daughters worse. The dam in years had th' advantage to be wicked, But they were so in her belly.
Lacy	I must tell you, With reverence to your wealth, I do begin To think you of the same leaven.
Plenty	Take my counsel,

'Tis safer for your credit to profess
Yourself a cuckold, and upon record,
Than say they are your daughters.

Frugal   You go too far, sir.

Lacy   They have so articl'd with us –

Plenty   And will not take us   30
For their husbands, but their slaves, and so aforehand
They do profess they'll use us.

Frugal   Leave this heat.
Though they are mine, I must tell you, the perverseness
Of their manners (which they did not take from me,
But from their mother) qualified, they deserve
Your equals.

Lacy   True, but what's bred in the bone
Admits no hope of cure.

Plenty   Though saints and angels
Were their physicians.

Frugal   You conclude too fast.

Plenty   God be wi'you. I'll travel three years, but I'll bury
This shame that lives upon me.

Lacy   [*to* LORD LACY]   With your licence,   40
I'll keep him company.

Lord Lacy   Who shall furnish you
For your expenses?

Plenty   He shall not need your help:
My purse is his. We were rivals, but now friends,
And will live and die so.

Lacy   Ere we go, I'll pay

My duty as a son.

Plenty   And till then, leave you.

Exeunt [Sir Maurice] LACY *and* PLENTY

Lord Lacy   They are strangely mov'd.

Frugal   What's wealth, accompanied
With disobedience in a wife and children?
My heart will break.

Lord Lacy   Be comforted, and hope better.
We'll ride abroad. The fresh air and discourse
May yield us new inventions.

Frugal   You are noble,   50
And shall in all things, as you please, command me.
                                                Exeunt

ACT 3, SCENE 1

Enter SHAVE'EM *and* SECRET

Secret	Dead doings, daughter.
Shave'em	Doings? Sufferings, mother:

Men have forgotten what doing is,
And such as have to pay for what they do
Are impotent or eunuchs.

Music[ians] come down

Secret You have a friend yet,
And a striker, too, I take it.

Shave'em Goldwire is so,
And come to me by stealth, and as he can steal, maintains me
In clothes, I grant. But alas, dame, what's one friend?
I would have a hundred: for every hour and use
And change of humour I am in, a fresh one.
'Tis a flock of sheep that makes a lean wolf fat,   10
And not a single lambkin. I am starv'd,
Starv'd in my pleasures. I know not what a coach is
To hurry me to the Burse or Old Exchange;
The neathouse for musk melons and the gardens
Where we traffic for asparagus are to me
In the other world.

Secret There are other places, lady,
Where you might find customers.

Shave'em You would have me foot it

	To the dancing of the ropes, sit a whole afternoon there	
	In expectation of nuts and pippins?	
	Gape 'round me, and yet not find a chapman	20
	That in courtesy will bid a chop of mutton	
	Or pint of drum-wine for me?	

Secret   You are so impatient,
But I can tell you news will comfort you
And the whole sisterhood.

Shave'em   What's that?

Secret   I am told
Two ambassadors are come over: a French monsieur
And a Venetian, one of the Clarissimi,
A hot-rein'd marmoset. Their followers,
For their country's honour, after a long vacation,
Will make a full term with us.

Shave'em   They indeed are
Our certain and best customers.   *Knock within*
                                        Who knocks there?   30

Ramble   [*within*] Open the door.

Secret   What are you?

Ramble   [*within*]   Ramble.

Scuffle   [*within*]   Scuffle.

Ramble   [*within*] Your constant visitants.

Shave'em   Let 'em not in.
I know 'em – swaggering, suburbian roarers,
Six-penny truckers.

Ramble   [*within*]   Down go all your windows,
And your neighbours too shall suffer.

Scuffle	[*within*]	Force the doors.

Secret   They are outlaws, mistress Shave'em, and there is
No remedy against 'em. What should you fear?
They are but men, lying at your close ward.
You have soil'd their betters.

Shave'em   Out, you bawd. You care not
Upon what desperate service you employ me,   40
Nor with whom, so you have your fee.

Secret   Sweet ladybird,
Sing a milder key.

                Enter RAMBLE *and* SCUFFLE

Scuffle   [*to* SHAVE'EM]   Are you grown proud?

Ramble   I knew you a waistcoateer in the garden alleys,
And would come to a sailor's whistle.

Secret   Good sir Ramble,
Use her not roughly. She is very tender.

Ramble   Rank and rotten, is she not?
      [SHAVE'EM] *draws her knife;* RAMBLE [*draws*]
      his sword

Shave'em   Your spital rogueships
Shall not make me so.

Secret   As you are a man, Squire Scuffle,
Step in between 'em. A weapon of that length
Was ne'er drawn in my house.

Shave'em   Let him come on.
I'll scour it in your guts, you dog!

Ramble   You brach,   50
Are you turn'd mankind? You forgot I gave you,

When we last join'd issue, twenty pound.

Shave'em   O'er night,
And kick'd it out of me in the morning. I was then
A novice, but I know to make my game now.
Fetch the constable.

*Enter [Young] GOLDWIRE like a justice of [the] peace, DING'EM
like a constable, the MUSICIANS like watchmen*

Secret   Ah, me! Here's one unsent for,
And a justice of peace, too.

Shave'em   I'll hang you both,
You rascals (I can but ride): you for the purse
You cut at Paul's at a sermon – I have smok'd you –
And you, for the bacon you took on the highway   59
From the poor market woman as she rode from Romford.

Ramble   Mistress Shave'em –

Scuffle   Mistress Secret, on our knees
We beg your pardon.

Ramble   Set a ransom on us.

Secret   We cannot stand trifling. If you mean to save them,
Shut them out at the back door.

Shave'em   First, for punishment,
They shall leave their cloaks behind 'em, and in sign
I am their sovereign and they my vassals,
For homage kiss my shoe-sole, rogues, and vanish.
                            Exeunt RAMBLE and SCUFFLE

[Young] GOLDWIRE and the rest discovered

Goldwire   My brave virago. The coast's clear.
                [*To musicians*] Strike up.

Shave'em	My Goldwire made a justice.
Secret	And your scout Turn'd constable, and the musicians watchmen. 70
Goldwire	We come not to fright you, but to make you merry. [*To musicians*] A light lavolta! *They dance*
Shave'em	I am tir'd. No more. [*To* GOLDWIRE] This was your device?
Ding'em	Wholly his own. He is No pig-sconce, mistress.
Secret	He has an excellent headpiece.
Goldwire	Fie, no, not I! Your jeering gallants say We citizens have no wit.
Ding'em	He dies that says so. This was a masterpiece.
Goldwire	A trifling stratagem, Not worth the talking of.
Shave'em	I must kiss thee for't, Again and again.
Ding'em	Make much of her. Did you know What suitors she had since she saw you?
Goldwire	I'the way of marriage?
Ding'em	Yes, sir, for marriage and the other thing, too: 81 The commodity is the same. An Irish lord offer'd her Five pound a week.
Secret	And a cashier'd captain half Of his entertainment.
Ding'em	And a new-made courtier

The next suit he could beg.

Goldwire   And did my sweet one
Refuse all this for me?

Shave'em   Weep not for joy,
'Tis true. Let others talk of lords and commanders
And country heirs for their servants, but give me
My gallant prentice. He parts with his money
So civilly and demurely, keeps no account   90
Of his expenses, and comes ever furnish'd.
I know thou has brought money to make up
My gown and petticoat with th' appurtenances.

Goldwire I have it here, duck. Thou shalt want for nothing.

Shave'em Let the chamber be perfum'd,
[*to* DING'EM]   and get you, sirrah,
His cap and pantables ready.

Goldwire   There's for thee,
And thee – that for a banquet.
                    [*Gives* DING'EM *and* SECRET *money*]

Secret   And a caudle
Against you rise.

Goldwire   There.   [*Gives more money*]

Shave'em   Usher us up in state.

Goldwire You will be constant?

Shave'em   Thou art the whole world to me.
                    Exeunt, wanton music played before 'em

ACT 3, SCENE 2

Enter LUKE

Anne	[*within*] Where is this uncle?
Lady Frugal	[*within*] Call this beadsman-brother:
	He hath forgot attendance.
Mary	[*within*] Seek him out:
	Idleness spoils him.
Luke	I deserve much more than

Their scorn can load me with, and 'tis but justice
That I should live the family's drudge, design'd
To all the sordid offices their pride
Imposes on me, since if I now sat
A judge in mine own cause, I should conclude
I am not worth their pity. Such as want
Discourse and judgement, and through weakness fall,   10
May merit man's compassion, but I –
That knew profuseness of expense the parent
Of wretched poverty (her fatal daughter) –
To riot out mine own, to live upon
The alms of others, steering on a rock
I might have shunn'd! O heaven, 'tis not fit
I should look upward, much less hope for mercy.

Enter LADY [FRUGAL], ANNE, MARY, STARGAZE *and* MILLICENT

Lady Frugal	What are you devising, sir?

Anne	My uncle is much
	Giv'n to his devotion.
Mary	And takes time to mumble
	A paternoster to himself.
Lady Frugal	[*to* LUKE] Know you where 20
	Your brother is? It better would become you
	(Your means of life depending wholly on him)
	To give your attendance.
Luke	In my will, I do,
	But since he rode forth yesterday with Lord Lacy,
	I have not seen him.
Lady Frugal	And why went not you
	By his stirrup? How do you look? Were his eyes clos'd,
	You'd be glad of such employment.
Luke	'Twas his pleasure
	I should wait your commands, and those I am ever
	Most ready to receive.
Lady Frugal	I know you can speak well,
	But say and do.

Enter LORD LACY *with a will*

Luke	Here comes my lord.
Lady Frugal	Further off: 30
	You are no companion for him, and his business
	Aims not at you, as I take it.
Luke	[*aside*] Can I live
	In this base condition?
Lady Frugal	[*to* LORD LACY] I hop'd, my lord,
	You had brought Master Frugal with you, for I must ask

An account of him from you.

Lord Lacy   I can give it, lady,
But with the best discretion of a woman
And a strong fortified patience, I desire you
To give it hearing.

Luke   My heart beats.

Lady Frugal   My lord,
You much amaze me.

Lord Lacy   I shall astonish you.
The noble merchant, who, living, was for his   40
Integrity and upright dealing (a rare
Miracle in a rich citizen), London's
Best honour is – I am loath to speak it –

Luke   Wondrous strange!

Lady Frugal   I do suppose the worst. Not dead,
I hope?

Lord Lacy   Your supposition's true, your hopes are false.
He's dead.

Lady Frugal   Ay, me!

Anne   My father!

Mary   My kind father!

Luke   Now they insult not.

Lord Lacy   Pray hear me out.
He's dead. Dead to the world and you, and now
Lives only to himself.

Luke   What riddle's this?

Lady Frugal   Act not the torturer in my afflictions,   50

But make me understand the sum of all
That I must undergo.

Lord Lacy   In a few words take it.
He is retir'd into a monastery,
Where he resolves to end his days.

Luke   More strange.

Lord Lacy   I saw him take post for Dover, and the wind
Sitting so fair, by this he's safe at Calais,
And ere long will be at Louvain.

Lady Frugal   Could I guess
What were the motives that induc'd him to it,
'Twere some allay to my sorrows.

Lord Lacy   I'll instruct you,
And chide you into that knowledge. 'Twas your pride
Above your rank, and stubborn disobedience   61
Of these your daughters, in their milk suck'd from you;
At home, the harshness of his entertainment,
You wilfully forgetting that your all
Was borrow'd from him; and to hear abroad
The imputations dispers'd upon you,
And justly too, I fear, that drew him to
This strict retirement. And thus much said for him,
I am myself to accuse you.

Lady Frugal   I confess
A guilty cause to him, but in a thought,   70
My lord, I ne'er wrong'd you.

Lord Lacy   In fact, you have.
The insolent disgrace you put upon
My only son and Master Plenty (men that lov'd

Your daughters in a noble way), to wash off
The scandal, put a resolution in 'em
For three years' travel.

Lady Frugal   I am much griev'd for it.

Lord Lacy   One thing I had forgot. Your rigour to
His decay'd brother, in which your flatteries,
Or sorceries, made him a coagent with you,
Wrought not the least impression.

Luke   Humph! This sounds well.

Lady Frugal 'Tis now past help. After these storms, my lord,   81
  A little calm, if you please.

Lord Lacy   If what I have told you
Show'd like a storm, what now I must deliver
Will prove a raging tempest. His whole estate
In lands and leases, debts and present moneys,
With all the movables he stood possess'd of,
With the best advice which he could get for gold
From his learned counsel, by this formal will
Is pass'd o'er to his brother. [*To* LUKE] With it take
The key of his counting house.
[*To* LADY FRUGAL]   Not a groat left you,   90
Which you could call your own.

Lady Frugal   Undone forever.

Anne & Mary What will become of us?

Luke   Humph!

Lord Lacy   The scene's chang'd,
And he that was your slave, by fate appointed
Your governour.
          [LADY FRUGAL, ANNE *and* MARY *kneel*]

                You kneel to me in vain:
I cannot help you; I discharge the trust
Impos'd upon me. This humility
From him may gain remission, and perhaps
Forgetfulness of your barbarous usage to him.

Lady Frugal   Am I come to this?

Lord Lacy   [*to* LUKE]   Enjoy your own, good sir,
But use it with due reverence. I once heard you   100
Speak most divinely in the opposition
Of a revengeful humour; to these, show it,
And such who then depended on the mercy
Of your brother, wholly now at your devotion,
And make good the opinion I held of you,
Of which I am most confident.

Luke   [*to* LADY FRUGAL, ANNE *and* MARY] Pray you, rise,
And rise with this assurance: I am still,
As I was of late, your creature, and – if rais'd
In any thing – 'tis in my power to serve you.   109
My will is still the same. [*To* LORD LACY] O my lord,
This heap of wealth which you possess me of –
Which to a worldly man had been a blessing,
And to the messenger might with justice challenge
A kind of adoration – is to me
A curse I cannot thank you for, and much less
Rejoice in that tranquillity of mind
My brother's vows must purchase. I have made
A dear exchange with him. He now enjoys
My peace and poverty, the trouble of
His wealth conferr'd on me, and that a burden   120
Too heavy for my weak shoulders.

Lord Lacy   Honest soul,

With what feeling he receives it!

Lady Frugal   You shall have
My best assistance, if you please to use it,
To help you to support it.

Luke   By no means.
The weight shall rather sink me than you part
With one short minute from those lawful pleasures
Which you were born to in your care to aid me.
You shall have all abundance. In my nature,
I was ever liberal – my lord, you know it –
Kind, affable. And now methinks I see   130
Before my face the jubilee of joy,
When it is assur'd my brother lives in me,
His debtors in full cups crown'd to my health,
With paeans to my praise will celebrate,
For they well know 'tis beyond me to take
The forfeiture of a bond. Nay, I shall blush,
The interest never paid after three years,
When I demand my principal. And his servants,
Who from a slavish fear paid their obedience
By him exacted, now when they are mine   140
Will grow familiar friends, and as such use me,
Being certain of the mildness of my temper,
Which my change of fortune, frequent in most men,
Hath not the power to alter.

Lord Lacy   Yet take heed, sir,
You ruin it not with too much lenity,
What his fit severity rais'd.

Lady Frugal   And we fall from
That height we have maintain'd.

Luke   I'll build it higher,

To admiration higher. With disdain
I look upon these habits, no way suiting
The wife and daughters of a knighted citizen   150
Bless'd with abundance.

Lord Lacy   There, sir, I join with you.
A fit decorum must be kept, the court
Distinguish'd from the city.

Luke   With your favour,
I know what you would say, but give me leave
In this to be your advocate. You are wide,
Wide the whole region, in what I purpose.
Since all the titles, honours, long descents
Borrow their gloss from wealth, the rich with reason
May challenge their prerogatives. And it shall be
My glory – nay, a triumph – to revive   160
In the pomp that these shall shine, the memory
Of the Roman matrons who kept captive queens
To be their handmaids.
[*To* LADY FRUGAL]   And when you appear
Like Juno in full majesty, and my nieces
Like Iris, Hebe, or what deities else
Old poets fancy (your cramm'd wardrobes richer
Than various natures), and draw down the envy
Of our western world upon you, only hold me
Your vigilant Hermes with aerial wings,
My caduceus my strong zeal to serve you,   170
Press'd to fetch in all rarities may delight you,
And I am made immortal.

Lord Lacy   A strange frenzy.

Luke   Off with these rags, and then to bed. There dream
Of future greatness, which when you awake,

	I'll make a certain truth. But I must be
	A doer, not a promiser. The performance
	Requiring haste, I kiss your hands and leave you.
	Exit LUKE
Lord Lacy	Are we all turn'd statues? Have his strange words
	charm'd us?
	What muse you on, lady?
Lady Frugal	Do not trouble me.
Lord Lacy	Sleep you too, young ones?
Anne	Swift wing'd time till now
	Was never tedious to me. Would 'twere night. 181
Mary	Nay, morning rather.
Lord Lacy	Can you ground your faith
	On such impossibilities?
	[*To* LADY FRUGAL] Have you so soon
	Forgot your good husband?
Lady Frugal	He was a vanity
	I must no more remember.
Lord Lacy	Excellent!
	You, your kind father?
Anne	Such an uncle never
	Was read of in story!
Lord Lacy	Not one word in answer
	Of my demands?
Mary	You are but a lord, and know
	My thoughts soar higher.
Lord Lacy	Admirable! I will leave you
	To your castles in the air. [*Aside*] When I relate this, 190

	It will exceed belief, but he must know it.
	Exit LORD LACY
Stargaze	Now I may boldly speak. May it please you, madam,
	To look upon your vassal? I foresaw this;
	The stars assur'd it.
Lady Frugal	I begin to feel
	Myself another woman.
Stargaze	Now you shall find
	All my predictions true, and nobler matches
	Prepar'd for my young ladies.
Millicent	Princely husbands.
Anne	I'll go no less.
Mary	Not a word more.
	Provide my night-rail.
Millicent	What shall we be tomorrow?
	Exeunt

ACT 3, SCENE 3

Enter LUKE *with a key*

Luke	'Twas no fantastic object, but a truth,
	A real truth. Nor dream: I did not slumber,
	And could wake ever with a brooding eye
	To gaze upon't! It did endure the touch.
	I saw and felt it. Yet what I beheld
	And handl'd oft, did so transcend belief
	(My wonder and astonishment pass'd o'er)
	I faintly could give credit to my senses.

[*To the key*] Thou dumb magician that without a charm
Did'st make my entrance easy, to possess   10
What wise men wish and toil for. Hermes' moly,
Sibylla's golden bough, the great elixir
(Imagin'd only by the alchemist),
Compar'd with thee are shadows, thou the substance
And guardian of felicity. No marvel
My brother made thy place of rest his bosom,
Thou being the keeper of his heart, a mistress
To be hugg'd ever. In by-corners of
This sacred room, silver in bags heap'd up
– Like billets saw'd and ready for the fire,   20
Unworthy to hold fellowship with bright gold
That flow'd about the room – conceal'd itself.
There needs no artificial light: the splendour
Makes a perpetual day there, night and darkness
By that still burning lamp forever banish'd.
But when guided by that, my eyes had made
Discovery of the caskets, and they open'd,
Each sparkling diamond from itself shot forth
A pyramid of flames, and in the roof
Fix'd it a glorious star and made the place   30
Heav'n's abstract or epitome. Rubies, sapphires
And ropes of orient pearl, these seen, I could not
But look on with contempt. And yet I found
What weak credulity could have no faith in
A treasure far exceeding these. Here lay
A manor bound fast in a skin of parchment,
The wax continuing hard, the acres melting.
Here, a sure deed of gift for a market town
If not redeem'd this day, which is not in
The unthrift's power – there being scarce one shire   40
In Wales or England where my moneys are not

Lent out at usury, the certain hook
To draw in more. I am sublim'd! Gross earth
Supports me not. I walk on air! – Who's there?
Thieves! Raise the street! Thieves!

Enter LORD [LACY *with*] Sir John [FRUGAL], [Sir Maurice]
LACY *and* PLENTY [*dressed*] *as Indians*

Lord Lacy   What strange passion's this?
Have you your eyes? Do you know me?

Luke   You, my lord,
I do, but this retinue, in these shapes too,
May well excuse my fears. When 'tis your pleasure
That I should wait upon you, give me leave
To do it at your own house, for I must tell you,   50
Things as they are now with me well consider'd,
I do not like such visitants.

Lord Lacy   Yesterday,
When you had nothing (praise your poverty for't),
You could have sung secure before a thief,
But now you are grown rich, doubts and suspicions
And needless fears possess you. Thank a good brother,
But let not this exalt you.

Luke   A good brother?
Good in his conscience, I confess, and wise
In giving o'er the world. But his estate
Which your lordship may conceive great, no way   60
Answers the general opinion. Alas,
With a great charge, I am left a poor man by him.

Lord Lacy A poor man, say you?

Luke   Poor, compar'd with what

'Tis thought I do possess. Some little land,
Fair household furniture, a few good debts,
But empty bags I find. Yet I will be
A faithful steward to his wife and daughters,
And to the utmost of my power, obey
His will in all things.

Lord Lacy   I'll not argue with you
Of his estate, but bind you to performance   70
Of his last request, which is for testimony
Of his religious charity, that you would
Receive these Indians, lately sent him from
Virginia, into your house, and labour
At any rate with the best of your endeavours,
Assisted by the aid of our divines,
To make 'em Christians.

Luke   Call you this, my lord,
Religious charity? To send infidels,
Like hungry locusts, to devour the bread
Should feed his family? I neither can,   80
Nor will, consent to't.

Lord Lacy   Do not slight it. 'Tis
With him a business of such consequence
That should he only hear 'tis not embrac'd,
And cheerfully (in this his conscience aiming
At the saving of three souls), 'twill draw him o'er
To see it himself accomplish'd.

Luke   Heav'n forbid
I should divert him from his holy purpose
To worldly cares again. I rather will
Sustain the burden, and with the converted
Feast the converters, who I know will prove   90

	The greater feeders.
Frugal	*Oh, ha, enewah Chrish bully leika.*
Plenty	*Enaula.*
Lacy	*Harrico botikia bonnery.*
Luke	Ha! In this heathen language How is it possible our doctors should Hold conference with 'em? Or I use the means For their conversion?

Lord Lacy   That shall be no hindrance
To your good purposes. They have liv'd long
In the English colony and speak our language   100
As their own dialect. The business does concern you;
Mine own designs command me hence. Continue
As in your poverty you were, a pious
And honest man.   *Exit* [LORD LACY]

Luke   That is, interpreted,
A slave and beggar.

Frugal   You conceive it right.
There being no religion nor virtue
But in abundance, and no vice but want,
All deities serve Plutus.

Luke   Oracle!

Frugal   Temples rais'd to ourselves in the increase
Of wealth and reputation, speak a wise man,   110
But sacrifice to an imagin'd power,
Of which we have no sense but in belief,
A superstitious fool.

Luke   True worldly wisdom.

Frugal   All knowledge else is folly.

Luke   Now we are yours.
                 Be confident your better angel is
                 Enter'd your house.

Plenty   There being nothing in
                 The compass of your wishes but shall end
                 In their fruition to the full.

Frugal   As yet,
                 You do not know us, but when you understand
                 The wonders we can do, and what the ends were   120
                 That brought us hither, you will entertain us
                 With more respect.

Luke   There's something whispers to me,
                 These are no common men. My house is yours:
                 Enjoy it freely. Only grant me this –
                 Not to be seen abroad till I have heard
                 More of your sacred principles. Pray, enter.
                 You are learned Europeans, and we worse
                 Than ignorant Americans.

Frugal   You shall find it.   *Exeunt*

Act 4, Scene 1

Enter DING'EM, GETALL *and* HOLDFAST

Ding'em	Not speak with him? With fear survey me better, Thou figure of famine.
Getall	Coming, as we do, From his quondam patrons, his dear ingles now, The brave spark Tradewell –
Ding'em	And the man of men In the service of a woman, gallant Goldwire.

Enter LUKE

Holdfast	I know 'em for his prentices without These flourishes. [*To* LUKE] Here are rude fellows, sir.
Ding'em	Not yours, you rascal!
Holdfast	No, don pimp: you may seek 'em In Bridewell or the hole. Here are none of your comrogues.
Luke	One of 'em looks as he would cut my throat. 10 Your business, friends?
Holdfast	I'll fetch a constable: Let him answer him in the stocks.
Ding'em	Stir an' thou dar'st. Fright me with Bridewell and the stocks? They are flea-bitings I am familiar with. [*He draws*]
Luke	Pray you, put up. [*To* HOLDFAST] And, sirrah, hold your peace.
Ding'em	Thy word's a law,

And I obey. [*To* HOLDFAST] Live, scrape-shoe, and
  be thankful.
[*To* LUKE] Thou man of muck and money (for as such
I now salute thee), the suburban gamesters
Have heard thy fortunes, and I am in person
Sent to congratulate.

Getall   The news hath reach'd   20
The ordinaries, and all the gamesters are
Ambitious to shake the golden golls
Of worshipful Master Luke. I come from Tradewell,
Your fine facetious factor.

Ding'em   I from Goldwire.
He and his Helen have prepar'd a banquet
With the appurtenances to entertain thee,
For (I must whisper in thine ear) thou art
To be her Paris. But bring money with thee
To quit old scores.

Getall   Blind chance hath frown'd upon
Brave Tradewell. He's blown up, but not without   30
Hope of recovery, so you supply him
With a good round sum. In my house, I can assure you,
There's half a million stirring.

Luke   What hath he lost?

Getall   Three hundred.

Luke   A trifle.

Getall   Make it up a thousand,
And I will fit him with such tools as shall
Bring in a myriad.

Luke   They know me well,
Nor need you use such circumstances for 'em.

	What's mine is theirs. They are my friends, not servants,
	But in their care to enrich me, and these courses
	The speeding means. Your name, I pray you?
Getall	Getall. 40
	I have been many years an ordinary keeper,
	My box my poor revenue.
Luke	Your name suits well
	With your profession. Bid him bear up; he shall not
	Sit long on Penniless Bench.
Getall	There spake an angel.
Luke	Know you Mistress Shave'em?
Getall	The pontifical punk?
Luke	The same. Let him meet me there some two hours hence,
	[*to* DING'EM] And tell Tom Goldwire I will then be with him,
	Furnish'd beyond his hopes, and let your mistress
	Appear in her best trim.
Ding'em	She will make thee young,
	Old Aeson. She is ever furnish'd with 50
	Medea's drugs, restoratives. I fly
	To keep 'em sober till thy worship come.
	They will be drunk with joy else.
Getall	I'll run with you.
	Exeunt DING'EM and GETALL
Holdfast	You will not do as you say, I hope.
Luke	Inquire not.
	I shall do what becomes me. *Knocking* [*within*]
	To the door.
	New visitants: what are they?

Holdfast   A whole batch, sir,
          Almost of the same leaven: your needy debtors,
          Penury, Fortune, Hoist.

Luke   They come to gratulate
          The fortune fall'n upon me.

Holdfast   Rather, sir,
          Like the others, to prey on you.

Luke   I am simple,   60
          They know my good nature. But let' em in, however.

Holdfast   All will come to ruin. I see beggary
          Already knocking at the door.   [*Crossing to door*]
                              You may enter,
          But use a conscience, and do not work upon
          A tender-hearted gentleman too much:
          'Twill show like charity in you.

               Enter FORTUNE, PENURY [*and*] HOIST

Luke   Welcome, friends.
          I know your hearts and wishes: you are glad
          You have chang'd your creditor.

Penury   I weep for joy
          To look upon his worship's face.

Fortune   His worship's?
          I see Lord Mayor written on his forehead,   70
          The cap of maintenance and city sword
          Borne up in state before him.

Hoist   Hospitals
          And a third Burse erected by his honour.

Penury   The city poet on the pageant day

Preferring him before Gresham.

Hoist   All the conduits
Spouting Canary sack.

Fortune   Not a prisoner left
Under ten pounds.

Penury   We, his poor beadsmen, feasting
Our neighbours on his bounty.

Luke   May I make good
Your prophecies, gentle friends, as I'll endeavour
To the utmost of my power.

Holdfast   Yes, for one year,   80
And break the next.

Luke   [to HOLDFAST]   You are ever prating, sirrah.
Your present business, friends?

Fortune   Were your brother present,
Mine had been of some consequence, but now
The power lies in your worship's hand, 'tis little,
And will I know, as soon as ask'd, be granted.

Luke   'Tis very probable.

Fortune   The kind forbearance
Of my great debt, by your means (heav'n prais'd for't),
Hath rais'd my sunk estate. I have two ships,
Which I long since gave lost, above my hopes
Return'd from Barbary, and richly freighted.   90

Luke   Where are they?

Fortune   Near Gravesend.

Luke   I am truly glad of't.

Fortune   I find your worship's charity, and dare swear so.

Now may I have your licence (as I know
With willingness I shall) to make the best
Of the commodities – though you have execution
And after judgement against all that's mine,
As my poor body – I shall be enabl'd
To make payment of my debts to all the world,
And leave myself a competence.

Luke   You much wrong me
If you only doubt it. [*To* HOIST] Yours, Master Hoist? 100

Hoist   'Tis the surrend'ring back the mortgage of
My lands, and on good terms, but three days' patience.
By an uncle's death, I have means left to redeem it
And cancel all the forfeited bonds I seal'd to
In my riots to the merchant, for I am
Resolv'd to leave off play and turn good husband.

Luke   A good intent, and to be cherish'd in you.
[*To* PENURY] Yours, Penury?

Penury   My state stands as it did, sir.
What I ow'd, I owe, but can pay nothing to you.
Yet if you please to trust me with ten pounds more,   110
I can buy a commodity of a sailor
Will make me a free man. There, sir, is his name,
And the parcels I am to deal for.   *Gives him a paper*

Luke   You are all so reasonable
In your demands that I must freely grant 'em.
Some three hours hence, meet me on the Exchange:
You shall be amply satisfied.

Penury   Heav'n preserve you.

Fortune   Happy were London if within her walls

She had many such rich men.

Luke   No more; now leave me.
                          Exeunt FORTUNE, HOIST *and* PENURY
I am full of various thoughts. Be careful, Holdfast,
I have much to do.

Holdfast   And I something to say,   120
Would you give me hearing.

Luke   At my better leisure.
'Till my return, look well unto the Indians.
In the meantime, do as this directs you.
[*Gives* HOLDFAST *the paper given him by* PENURY.] *Exeunt*

ACT 4, SCENE 2

Enter [Young] GOLDWIRE, [Young] TRADEWELL, SHAVE'EM,
SECRET, GETALL *and* DING'EM

Goldwire   'All that is mine is theirs.' Those were his words?

Ding'em   I am authentical.

Tradewell   And that I should not
Sit long on Penniless Bench?

Getall   But suddenly start up,
A gamester at the height, and cry 'At all!'.

Shave'em   And did he seem to have an inclination
To toy with me?

Ding'em   He wish'd you would put on
Your best habiliments, for he resolv'd
To make a jovial day on't.

Goldwire   Hug him close, wench,
                And thou may'st eat gold and amber. I well know him
                For a most insatiate drabber. He hath given,   10
                Before he spent his own estate (which was
                Nothing to the huge mass he's now possessed of),
                A hundred pound a leap.

Shave'em   Hell take my doctor!
                He should have brought me some fresh oil of talc;
                These ceruses are common.

Secret   Troth, sweet lady,
                The colours are well laid on.

Goldwire   And thick enough:
                I find that on my lips.

Shave'em   Do you so, Jack Sauce?
                I'll keep 'em further off.

Goldwire   Be assur'd first
                Of a new maintainer ere you cashier the old one.
                But bind him fast by thy sorceries and thou shalt   20
                Be my revenue, the whole college study
                The reparation of thy ruin'd face.
                Thou shalt have thy proper and bald-headed coachman;
                Thy tailor and embroiderer shall kneel
                To thee, their idol. Cheapside and the Exchange
                Shall court thy custom, and thou shalt forget
                There ever was a St Martin's. Thy procurer
                Shall be sheath'd in velvet, and a reverend veil
                Pass her for a grave matron. Have an eye to the door,
                And let loud music, when this monarch enters,   30
                Proclaim his entertainment.

Ding'em   That's my office.

Cornets flourish

The consort's ready.

Enter LUKE

Tradewell	And the god of pleasure,
	Master Luke, our Comus, enters.

Goldwire   [*to* SHAVE'EM]   Set your face in order:
I will prepare him. [*To* LUKE] Live I to see this day
And to acknowledge you my royal master?

Tradewell   Let the iron chests fly open, and the gold –
Rusty for want of use – appear again.

Getall   Make my ordinary flourish!

Shave'em   Welcome, sir,
To your own palace.   *Music*

Goldwire   Kiss your Cleopatra,
And show yourself in your magnificent bounties   40
A second Antony.

Ding'em   All the nine worthies.

Secret   Variety of pleasures wait on you,
And a strong back.

Luke   Give me leave to breathe, I pray you.
I am astonish'd. All this preparation
For me? And this choice modest beauty wrought
To feed my appetite?

All   We are all your creatures.

Luke   [*looking around*] A house well furnish'd.

Goldwire   At your own cost, sir;
Glad I, the instrument. I prophesied
You should possess what now you do, and therefore

	Prepar'd it for your pleasure. There's no rag	50
	This Venus wears, but on my knowledge was	
	Deriv'd from your brother's cash. The lease of the house	
	And furniture cost near a thousand, sir.	

Shave'em But now you are master both of it and me,
           I hope you'll build elsewhere.

Luke   And see you plac'd,
           Fair one, to your desert. As I live, friend Tradewell,
           I hardly knew you, your clothes so well become you.
           What is your loss? Speak truth.

Tradewell   Three hundred, sir.

Getall   But on a new supply, he shall recover
           The sum twenty times o'er.

Shave'em [*to* LUKE]   There is a banquet,   60
           And after that, a soft couch that attends you.

Luke   I couple not in the daylight. Expectation
           Heightens the pleasure of the night, my sweet one.
           Your music's harsh. Discharge it. I have provided
           A better consort, and you shall frolick it
           In another place.   *Cease music*

Goldwire   But have you brought gold and store, sir?

Tradewell I long to 'ware the caster'.

Goldwire   I to appear
           In a fresh habit.

Shave'em   My mercer and my silkman
           Waited me two hours since.

Luke   I am no porter
           To carry so much gold as will supply   70

Your vast desires, but I have ta'en order for you.

Enter SHERIFF, MARSHAL *and* OFFICERS

You shall have what is fitting, and they come here
Will see it perform'd.
[*To* SHERIFF]   Do your offices: you have
My Lord Chief Justice's warrant for't.

Sheriff	Seize 'em all!
Shave'em	The city marshal!
Goldwire	And the sheriff! I know him.
Secret	We are betray'd.
Ding'em	Undone.
Getall	Dear Master Luke.

Goldwire   You cannot be so cruel. Your persuasion
Chid us into these courses, oft repeating,
'Show yourself city sparks, and hang up money'.

Luke   True, when it was my brother's, I contemn'd it,   80
But now it is mine own, the case is alter'd.

Tradewell Will you prove yourself a devil? Tempt us to mischief
And then discover it?

Luke   Argue that hereafter.
[*To* GOLDWIRE] In the meantime, Master Goldwire –
    you that made
Your ten pound suppers, kept your punks at livery
In Brentford, Staines and Barnet, and this in London,
Held correspondence with your fellow cashiers,
'Ka me, ka thee', and knew in your accounts
To cheat my brother – if you can, evade me.
[*To both*] If there be law in London, your fathers' bonds   90

Shall answer for what you are out.

Goldwire   You often told us
It was a bugbear.

Luke   Such a one as shall fright 'em
Out of their estates to make me satisfaction
To the utmost scruple. And for you, madam,
My Cleopatra, by your own confession,
Your house and all your movables are mine.
Nor shall you nor your matron need to trouble
Your mercer or your silkman. A blue gown
And a whip to boot (as I will handle it)
Will serve the turn in Bridewell, and these soft hands,   100
When they are inur'd to beating hemp, be scour'd
In your penitent tears, and quite forget
Powders and bitter almonds.

Shave'em,
Secret &   Will you show no mercy?
Ding'em

Luke   I am inexorable.

Getall   I'll make bold
To take my leave. The gamesters stay my coming.

Luke   We must not part so, gentle Master Getall.
Your box, your certain income, must pay back
Three hundred, as I take it, or you lie by it.
There's a half a million stirring in your house:
This is a poor trifle. Master Sheriff and Master Marshal,   110
On your perils, do your offices.

Goldwire   [*to* LUKE]   Dost thou cry now
Like a maudlin gamester after loss? I'll suffer
Like a Roman, and now in my misery –

In scorn of all thy wealth – to thy teeth tell thee,
Thou wert my pander.

Luke   Shall I hear this from
My prentice?

Marshal   Stop his mouth.

Sheriff   Away with 'em.
                                  Exeunt [all except LUKE]

Luke   A prosperous omen in my entrance to
             My alter'd nature. These house thieves remov'd
             And what was lost, beyond my hopes recover'd,
             Will add unto my heap. Increase of wealth   120
             Is the rich man's ambition, and mine
             Shall know no bounds. The valiant Macedon,
             Having in his conceit subdued one world,
             Lamented that there were no more to conquer.
             In my way, he shall be my great example,
             And when my private house in cramm'd abundance
             Shall prove the chamber of the city poor,
             And Genoese bankers shall look pale with envy
             When I am mention'd, I shall grieve there is
             No more to be exhausted in one kingdom.   130
             Religion, conscience, charity: farewell.
             To me you are words only, and no more.
             All human happiness consists in store.   *Exit*

ACT 4, SCENE 3

Enter [three] SERGEANTS, FORTUNE, HOIST [*and*] PENURY

Fortune	At Master Luke's suit? The action twenty thousand?
1 Sergeant	With two or three executions, which shall grind You to powder when we have you in the Counter.
Fortune	Thou dost belie him, varlet. He, good gentleman, Will weep when he hears how we are us'd.
1 Sergeant	Yes, millstones.
Penury	He promis'd to lend me ten pounds for a bargain: He will not do it this way.

2 Sergeant   I have warrant
For what I have done. You are a poor fellow
And, there being little to be got by you,
In charity (as I am an officer),   10
I would not have seen you, but upon compulsion,
And for mine own security.

3 Sergeant   You are a gallant,
And I do you a courtesy, provided
That you have money. For a piece an hour,
I'll keep you in the house till you send for bail.

2 Sergeant   [*to* 1 SERG.] In the meantime, yeoman, run to the other Counter
And search if there be aught else out against him.

3 Sergeant   That done, haste to his creditors. [*Exit* 1 SERGEANT]
                                      He's a prize,
And as we are city pirates, by our oaths,
We must make the best on't.

Hoist   Do your worst. I care not.

	I'll be remov'd to the Fleet, and drink and drab there 21
	In spite of your teeth. I now repent I ever
	Intended to be honest.

Enter LUKE

3 Sergeant	Here he comes
	You had best tell so.
Fortune	Worshipful sir,
	You come in time to free us from these bandogs.
	I know you gave no way to't.
Penury	Or if you did,
	'Twas but to try our patience.
Hoist	I must tell you,
	I do not like such trials.
Luke	Are you sergeants
	Acquainted with the danger of a rescue,
	Yet stand here prating in the street? The Counter 30
	Is a safer place to parley in.
Fortune	Are you in earnest?
Luke	Yes, faith, I will be satisfied to a token,
	Or build upon't, you rot there.
Fortune	Can a gentleman
	Of your soft and silken temper speak such language?
Penury	So honest, so religious?
Hoist	That preach'd
	So much of charity for us to your brother?
Luke	Yes, when I was in poverty, it show'd well,
	But I inherit with his state, his mind
	And rougher nature. I grant, then I talk'd

	(For some ends to myself conceal'd) of pity, 40

       (For some ends to myself conceal'd) of pity,   40
The poor man's orisons, and such like nothing.
But what I thought, you all shall feel, and with rigour.
Kind Master Luke says it.
[*To* SERGEANTS]   Who pays for your attendance?
Do you wait *gratis*?

Fortune   Hear us speak.

Luke   While I,
Like the adder, stop mine ears. Or did I listen,
Though you spake with the tongues of angels to me,
I am not to be alter'd.

Fortune   Let me make the best
Of my ships and their freight.

Penury   Lend me the ten pounds you promis'd.

Hoist   A day or two's patience to redeem my mortgage,
And you shall be satisfied.

Fortune   To the utmost farthing.   50

Luke   I'll show some mercy, which is, that I will not
Torture you with false hopes, but make you know
What you shall trust to. [*To* FORTUNE] Your ships to my use
Are seiz'd on. [*To* PENURY] I have got into my hands
Your bargains from the sailor ('twas a good one
For such a petty sum). [*To* HOIST] I will likewise take
The extremity of your mortgage and the forfeit
Of your several bonds; the use and principal
Shall not serve. Think of the basket, wretches,
And a coal sack for a winding sheet.

Fortune   Broker!   60

Hoist   Jew!

Fortune	Imposter!
Hoist	Cut-throat!
Fortune	Hypocrite!
Luke	Do, rail on.
	Move mountains with your breath: it shakes not me.
Penury	[*kneeling*] On my knees I beg compassion. My wife and children
	Shall hourly pray for your worship.
Fortune	Mine betake thee
	To the devil thy tutor.
Penury	Look upon my tears.
Hoist	My rage.
Fortune	My wrongs.
Luke	They are all alike to me:
	Entreats, curses, prayers or imprecations.
	[*To sergeants*] Do your duties, sergeants: I am elsewhere look'd for.
	Exit LUKE

3 Sergeant	This your kind creditor?	
2 Sergeant	A vast villain, rather.	
Penury	See, see, the sergeants pity us, yet he's marble.	70
Hoist	Buried alive!	
Fortune	There's no means to avoid it. *Exeunt*	

ACT 4, SCENE 4

Enter HOLDFAST, STARGAZE *and* MILLICENT

Stargaze	Not wait upon my lady?
Holdfast	Nor come at her.

Stargaze   Not wait upon my lady?

Holdfast   Nor come at her.
You find it not in your almanac.

Millicent   Nor I have licence
To bring her breakfast?

Holdfast   My new master hath
Decreed this for a fasting day. She hath feasted long,
And after a carnival, Lent ever follows.

Millicent   Give me the key of her wardrobe. You'll repent this –
I must know what gown she'll wear.

Holdfast   You are mistaken,
Dame president of the sweetmeats. She and her daughters
Are turn'd philosophers, and must carry all
Their wealth about 'em. They have clothes laid in their chamber,
If they please to put 'em on, and without help too,   11
Or they may walk naked. [*To* STARGAZE] You look,
  Master Stargaze,
As you had seen a strange comet, and had now foretold
The end of the world, and on what day.
[*To* MILLICENT]   And you,
As the wasps had broke into the gallipots
And eaten up your apricots.

Lady Frugal [*within*]   Stargazer! Millicent!

Millicent   My lady's voice!

Holdfast   Stir not, you are confin'd here.

[*To* LADY FRUGAL] Your ladyship may approach them,
   if you please,
But they are bound in this circle.

Lady Frugal	[*within*] Mine own bees

Rebel against me. When my kind brother knows this,   20
I will be so reveng'd –

Holdfast   The world's well alter'd.
He's your kind brother now, but yesterday,
Your slave and jesting-stock.

Enter LADY [FRUGAL], ANNE [*and*] MARY, *in coarse habit, weeping*

Millicent   What witch hath transform'd you?

Stargaze   Is this the glorious shape your cheating brother
Promis'd you should appear in?

Millicent   My young ladies
In buffin gowns and green aprons! Tear 'em off!
Rather show all than be seen thus.

Holdfast   'Tis more comely,
Iwis, than their other whim-whams.

Millicent   A French hood, too.
Now 'tis out of fashion, a fool's cap would show better.   29

Lady Frugal   We are fool'd indeed. By whose command are we us'd thus?

Enter LUKE

Holdfast   Here he comes that can best resolve you.

Lady Frugal   O good brother,
Do you thus preserve your protestation to me?
Can queens envy this habit, or did Juno
E'er feast in such a shape?

Anne   You talk'd of Hebe,

	Of Iris, and I know not what, but were they
	Dress'd as we are? They were sure some chandler's daughters,
	Bleaching linen in Moorfields.
Mary	Or Exchange wenches,
	Coming from eating pudding pies on a Sunday
	At Pimlico or Islington.
Luke	[*to* LADY FRUGAL] Save you, sister.

I now dare style you so, for you were before   40
Too glorious to be look'd on. Now you appear
Like a city matron, and my pretty nieces
Such things as were born and bred there. Why should you ape
The fashions of court ladies, whose high titles
And pedigrees of long descent give warrant
For their superfluous bravery? 'Twas monstrous.
Till now you ne'er look'd lovely.

Lady Frugal   Is this spoken
In scorn?

Luke   Fie, no! With judgement. I make good
My promise and now show you like yourselves,
In your own natural shapes, and stand resolv'd   50
You shall continue so.

Lady Frugal   It is confess'd, sir.

Luke   'Sir'? 'Sirrah': use your old phrase. I can bear it.

Lady Frugal That, if you please, forgotten. We acknowledge
We have deserv'd ill from you, yet despair not;
Though we are at your disposure, you'll maintain us
Like your brother's wife and daughters.

Luke   'Tis my purpose.

Lady Frugal And not make us ridiculous?

Luke   Admir'd, rather,
          As fair examples for our proud city dames
          And their proud brood to imitate. Do not frown.
          If you do, I laugh, and glory that I have   60
          The power in you to scourge a general vice
          And rise up a new satirist. But hear gently,
          And in gentle phrase I'll reprehend
          Your late disguis'd deformity, and cry up
          This decency and neatness with th'advantage
          You shall receive by't.

Lady Frugal   We are bound to hear you.

Luke   With a soul inclin'd to learn. Your father was
          An honest country farmer, Goodman Humble,
          By his neighbours ne'er called 'Master'. Did your pride
          Descend from him? But let that pass. Your fortune –   70
          Or rather, your husband's industry – advanc'd you
          To the rank of a merchant's wife. He made a knight,
          And your sweet mistress-ship ladyfied, you wore
          Satin on solemn days, a chain of gold,
          A velvet hood, rich borders, and sometimes
          A dainty miniver cap, a silver pin
          Headed with a pearl worth threepence, and thus far
          You were privileg'd, and no man envied it,
          It being for the city's honour that
          There should be a distinction between   80
          The wife of a patrician and plebeian.

Millicent Pray you, leave preaching, or choose some other text.
          Your rhetoric is too moving, for it makes
          Your auditory weep.

Luke   Peace, chattering magpie,

I'll treat of you anon. [*To* LADY FRUGAL] But when the height
And dignity of London's blessings grew
Contemptible, and the name 'Lady Mayoress'
Became a by-word, and you scorn'd the means
By which you were rais'd (my brother's fond indulgence
Giving the reins to't), and no object pleas'd you   90
But the glitt'ring pomp and bravery of the court,
What a strange – nay, monstrous – metamorphosis follow'd!
No English workman then could please your fancy;
The French and Tuscan dress your whole discourse;
[*gesturing to* MILLICENT] This bawd to prodigality entertain'd
To buzz into your ears what shape this countess
Appear'd in the last masque and how it drew
The young lords' eyes upon her;
[*gesturing to* STARGAZE]   and this usher
Succeeded in the eldest prentice's place
To walk before you.

Lady Frugal   Pray you, end.

Holdfast   Proceed, sir.   100
I could fast almost a prenticeship to hear you,
You touch 'em so to the quick.

Luke   Then, as I said,
The reverend hood cast off, your borrow'd hair,
Powder'd and curl'd, was by your dresser's art
Form'd like a coronet, hang'd with diamonds
And the richest orient pearl; your carcanets
That did adorn your neck of equal value;
Your Hungerland bands and Spanish *quellio* ruffs;
Great lords and ladies feasted to survey
Embroider'd petticoats, and sickness feign'd   110
That your night-rails of forty pounds apiece

	Might be seen with envy of the visitants;

Might be seen with envy of the visitants;
Rich pantables in ostentation shown,
And roses worth a family. You were serv'd in plate;
Stirr'd not a foot without your coach; and going
To church (not for devotion, but to show
Your pomp), you were tickl'd when the beggars cried,
'Heaven save your honour' – this idolatry
Paid to a painted room.

Holdfast [*to the women*]   Nay, you have reason
To blubber, all of you.

Luke   And when you lay   120
In childbed, at the christ'ning of this minx
(I well remember it), as you had been
An absolute princess, since they have no more,
Three several chambers hung: the first with arras
(And that for waiters); the second, crimson satin
For the meaner sort of guests; the third, of scarlet
Of the rich Tyrian dye; a canopy
To cover the brat's cradle; you in state
Like Pompey's Julia.

Lady Frugal   No more, I pray you.

Luke Of this be sure you shall not. I'll cut off   130
Whatever is exorbitant in you
Or in your daughters, and reduce you to
Your natural forms and habits, not in revenge
Of your base usage of me, but to fright
Others by your example. 'Tis decreed
You shall serve one another, for I will
Allow no waiter to you. [*To* HOLDFAST] Out of doors
With these useless drones.

Whilst the act plays, the footstep, little table, and arras hung up
for the musicians [to play behind]

Holdfast	[*to* STARGAZE *and* MILLICENT] Will you pack?
Millicent	Not till I have My trunks along with me.
Luke	Not a rag. You came Hither without a box.
Stargaze	You'll show to me, 140 I hope, sir, more compassion.
Holdfast	Troth, I'll be Thus far a suitor to him: he hath printed An almanac for this year at his own charge. Let him have th' impression with him to set up with.
Luke	For once I'll be entreated. Let it be Thrown to him out of the window.
Stargaze	O, cursed stars That reign'd at my nativity! How you have cheated Your poor observer.
Anne	Must we part in tears?
Mary	Farewell, good Millicent.
Lady Frugal	I am sick and meet with A rough physician. O, my pride and scorn, 150 How justly am I punish'd!
Mary	Now we suffer For our stubbornness and disobedience To our good father.
Anne	And the base conditions We impos'd upon our suitors.

Luke   Get you in,
          And caterwaul in a corner.

Lady Frugal   There's no contending.

          LADY [FRUGAL], ANNE, MARY *go off at one door*;
                    STARGAZE *and* MILLICENT *at the other*

Luke   How lik'st thou my carriage, Holdfast?

Holdfast   Well, in some part,
          But it relishes, I know not how, a little
          Of too much tyranny.

Luke   Thou art a fool.
          He's cruel to himself that dares not be   159
          Severe to those that us'd him cruelly.   *Exeunt*

ACT 5, SCENE 1

Enter LUKE [*with*] Sir John [FRUGAL], [Sir Maurice] LACY
and PLENTY [*as Indians*]

Luke	You care not, then, as it seems, to be converted To our religion?
Frugal	We know no such word Nor power but the devil, and him we serve for fear, Not love.
Luke	I am glad that charge is sav'd.
Frugal	We put That trick upon your brother to have means To come to the city. Now to you we'll discover The close design that brought us, with assurance If you lend your aids to furnish us with that Which in the colony was not to be purchas'd, No merchant ever made such a return For his most precious venture as you shall Receive from us – far, far above your hopes Or fancy to imagine.

Musicians come down to make ready for the song at [*the*] *arras*

10

Luke	It must be Some strange commodity, and of a dear value – Such an opinion is planted in me You will deal fairly – that I would not hazard. Give me the name of't.
Lacy	I fear you will make Some scruple in your conscience to grant it.
Luke	Conscience! No, no, so it may be done with safety

And without danger of the law.

Plenty   For that   20
You shall sleep securely. Nor shall it diminish,
But add unto your heap such an increase
As what you now possess shall appear an atom
To the mountain it brings with it.

Luke   Do not rack me
With expectation.

Frugal   Thus, then, in a word:
The devil. Why start you at his name? If you
Desire to wallow in wealth and worldly honours,
You must make haste to be familiar with him.
This devil – whose priest I am, and by him made
A deep magician (for I can do wonders) –   30
Appear'd to me in Virginia and commanded
With many stripes (for that's his cruel custom)
I should provide on pain of his fierce wrath
Against the next great sacrifice (at which
We, grovelling on our faces, fall before him),
Two Christian virgins, that with their pure blood
Might dye his horrid altars, and a third
(In his hate to such embraces as are lawful)
Married, and with your ceremonious rites,
As an oblation unto Hecate   40
And wanton lust, her favourite.

Luke   A devilish custom!
And yet why should it startle me? There are
Enough of the sex fit for this use, but virgins
And such a matron as you speak of, hardly
To be wrought to it.

Plenty   A mine of gold for a fee

	Waits him that undertakes it and performs it.	

Lacy   Know you no distress'd widow, or poor
          Maids, whose want of dower, though well born,
          Makes 'em weary of their own country?

Frugal   Such as had rather be
          Miserable in another world, than where   50
          They have surfeited in felicity?

Luke   Give me leave;
          I would not lose this purchase. [*Aside*] A grave matron
          And two pure virgins? Umph! I think my sister,
          Though proud, was ever honest, and my nieces
          Untainted yet. Why should not they be shipp'd
          For this employment? They are burdensome to me,
          And eat too much, and if they stay in London,
          They will find friends that to my loss will force me
          To composition. 'Twere a masterpiece
          If this could be effected. They were ever   60
          Ambitious of title. Should I urge,
          Matching with these, they shall live Indian queens?
          It may do much. But what shall I feel here,
          Knowing to what they are design'd? They absent,
          The thought of them will leave me. It shall be so.
          – I'll furnish you, and to endear the service,
          In mine own family and my blood, too.

Frugal Make this good and your house shall not contain
          The gold we'll send you.

Luke   You have seen my sister
          And my two nieces?

Frugal   Yes, sir.

Luke   These persuaded   70

How happily they shall live, and in what pomp,
When they are in your kingdoms, for you must
Work 'em a belief that you are kings –

Plenty   We are so.

Luke   I'll put it in practice instantly. Study you
For moving language. Sister! Nieces!

   Enter LADY [FRUGAL], ANNE [*and*] MARY

                                          How!
Still mourning? Dry your eyes, and clear these clouds
That do obscure your beauties. Did you believe
My personated reprehension, though
It show'd like a rough anger, could be serious?
Forget the fright I put you in. My end   80
In humbling you was to set off the height
Of honour, principal honour, which my studies,
When you least expect it, shall confer upon you.
Still you seem doubtful. Be not wanting to
Yourselves, nor let the strangeness of the means,
With the shadow of some danger, render you
Incredulous.

Lady Frugal   Our usage hath been such
As we can faintly hope that your intents
And language are the same.

Luke   I'll change those hopes
To certainties.

Frugal   [*aside*]   With what art he winds about them!   90

Luke   What will you say? Or what thanks shall I look for
If now I raise you to such eminence as
The wife and daughters of a citizen
Never arriv'd at? Many for their wealth, I grant,

	Have written 'ladies of honour', and some few	
	Have higher titles, and that's the farthest rise	
	You can in England hope for. What think you	
	If I should mark you out a way to live	
	Queens in another climate?	

Anne   We desire
A competence.

Mary   And prefer our country's smoke   100
Before outlandish fire.

Lady Frugal   But should we listen
To such impossibilities, 'tis not in
The power of man to make it good.

Luke   I'll do't,
Nor is this feat of majesty far remov'd:
It is but to Virginia.

Lady Frugal   How! Virginia!
High heav'n forbid! Remember, sir, I beseech you,
What creatures are shipp'd thither.

Anne   Condemn'd wretches,
Forfeited to the law.

Mary   Strumpets and bawds,
For the abomination of their life,
Spew'd out of their own country.

Luke   Your false fears   110
Abuse my noble purposes. Such indeed
Are sent as slaves to labour there, but you
To absolute sovereignty. Observe these men;
With reverence observe them. They are kings,
Kings of such spacious territories and dominions
As our great Britain measur'd will appear

A garden to't.

Lacy   You shall be ador'd there
As goddesses.

Frugal   Your litters made of gold
Supported by your vassals, proud to bear
The burden on their shoulders.

Plenty   Pomp and ease,   120
With delicates that Europe never knew,
Like pages shall wait on you.

Luke   If you have minds
To entertain the greatness offer'd to you,
With outstretched arms and willing hands embrace it.
But this refus'd, imagine what can make you
Most miserable here, and rest assur'd,
In storms it falls upon you.
[To Sir Maurice LACY and PLENTY] Take 'em in
And use your best persuasion. If that fail,
I'll send 'em aboard in a dry fat.
                    Exeunt [Sir Maurice] LACY, PLENTY,
                    LADY [FRUGAL], ANNE [and] MARY

Frugal   Be not mov'd, sir.
We'll work 'em to your will, yet ere we part,   130
Your worldly cares deferr'd, a little mirth
Would not misbecome us.

Luke   You say well. And now
It comes into my memory, this is my birthday,
Which with solemnity I would observe,
But that it would ask cost.

Frugal   That shall not grieve you.
By my art I will prepare you such a feast

As Persia in her height of pomp and riot
Did never equal, and ravishing music
As the Italian princes seldom heard
At their greatest entertainments. Name your guests.   140

Luke   I must have none.

Frugal   Not the city senate?

Luke   No.
Nor yet poor neighbours. The first would argue me
Of foolish ostentation, the latter
Of too much hospitality and a virtue
Grown obsolete and useless. I will sit
Alone and surfeit in my store (while others
With envy pine at it), my genius pamper'd
With the thought of what I am, and what they suffer
I have mark'd out to misery.

Frugal   You shall,
And something I will add you yet conceive not,   150
Nor will I be slow-pac'd.

Luke   I have one business,
And that dispatch'd, I am free.

Frugal   About it, sir:
Leave the rest to me.

Luke   Till now I ne'er lov'd magic.
                                    Exeunt

ACT 5, SCENE 2

Enter LORD [LACY], OLD GOLDWIRE *and* OLD TRADEWELL

Lord Lacy	Believe me, gentlemen, I never was
	So cozen'd in a fellow. He disguis'd
	Hypocrisy in such a cunning shape
	Of real goodness that I would have sworn
	This devil a saint. Master Goldwire and Master Tradewell,
	What do you mean to do? Put on.
Old Goldwire	With your lordship's favour.
Lord Lacy	I'll have it so.
Old Tradew.	Your will, my lord, excuses
	The rudeness of our manners.
Lord Lacy	You have receiv'd
	Penitent letters from your sons, I doubt not?
Old Tradew.	They are our only sons.
Old Goldw.	And, as we are fathers, 10
	Rememb'ring the errors of our youth,
	We would pardon slips in them.
Old Tradew.	And pay for 'em
	In a moderate way.
Old Goldw.	In which we hope your lordship
	Will be our mediator.
Lord Lacy	All my power
	You freely shall command.

Enter LUKE [*sumptuously dressed*]

'Tis he!

[*To* LUKE]   You are well met,
And to my wish – and wondrous brave! Your habit
Speaks you a merchant royal.

Luke   What I wear,
I take not upon trust.

Lord Lacy   Your betters may,
And blush not for't.

Luke   If you have nought else with me
But to argue that, I will make bold to   20
Leave you.

Lord Lacy   You are very peremptory.
Pray you, stay. I once held you an upright,
Honest man.

Luke   I am honester now by
A hundred thousand pound (I thank my stars for't)
Upon the Exchange, and if your late opinion
Be alter'd, who can help it? Good my lord,
To the point. I have other business than to talk
Of honesty and opinions.

Lord Lacy   Yet you may
Do well, if you please, to show the one, and merit
The other from good men, in a case that now   30
Is offer'd to you.

Luke   What is't? I am troubl'd.

Lord Lacy   Here are two gentlemen, the fathers of
Your brother's prentices.

Luke   Mine, my lord, I take it.

Lord Lacy   Master Goldwire and Master Tradewell.

Luke	They are welcome, if

They come prepar'd to satisfy the damage
I have sustain'd by their sons.

Old Goldw.	We are, so you please

To use a conscience.

Old Tradew.	Which we hope you will do,

For your own worship's sake.

Luke	Conscience, my friends,

And wealth are not always neighbours. Should I part
With what the law gives me, I should suffer mainly   40
In my reputation, for it would convince me
Of indiscretion. Nor will you, I hope, move me
To do myself such prejudice.

Lord Lacy	No moderation?

Luke   They cannot look for't and preserve in
Me a thriving citizen's credit. Your bonds lie
For your sons' truth, and they shall answer all
They have run out. The masters never prosper'd
Since gentlemen's sons grew prentices. When we look
To have our business done at home, they are
Abroad in the tennis court or in Partridge Alley,   50
In Lambeth Marsh, or a cheating ordinary,
Where I found your sons. I have your bonds. Look to't.
A thousand pounds apiece, and that will hardly
Repair my losses.

Lord Lacy	Thou dar'st not show thyself

Such a devil.

Luke	Good words.

Lord Lacy	Such a cut-throat. I have heard of

The usage of your brother's wife and daughters.

You shall find you are not lawless, and that your
Moneys cannot justify your villainies.

Luke   I endure this,
And, good my lord, now you talk in time of moneys,
Pay in what you owe me, and give me leave to wonder   60
Your wisdom should have leisure to consider
The business of these gentlemen or my carriage
To my sister or my nieces, being yourself
So much in my danger.

Lord Lacy   In thy danger?

Luke   Mine.
I find in my counting-house a manor pawn'd,
Pawn'd, my good lord – Lacy Manor – and that manor
From which you have the title of a lord,
An' it please your good lordship. You are a nobleman:
Pray you pay in my moneys. The interest
Will eat faster in't than aquafortis in iron.   70
Now, though you bear me hard, I love your lordship.
I grant your person to be privileg'd
From all arrests. Yet there lives a foolish creature
Call'd an under-sheriff, who – being well paid – will serve
An extent on lords', or lowns', land. Pay it in:
I would be loath your name should sink, or that
Your hopeful son, when he returns from travel,
Should find you, my lord, without land. You are angry
For my good counsel. Look you to your bonds: had I known
Of your coming, believe it, I would have had sergeants ready.
Lord, how you fret! But that a tavern's near,   81
You should taste a cup of muscadine in my house
To wash down sorrow, but there it will do better.
I know you'll drink a health to me.   *Exit* LUKE

Lord Lacy	To thy damnation.
	Was there ever such a villain? Heav'n forgive me
	For speaking so unchristianly, though he deserves it.
Old Goldw.	We are undone.
Old Tradew.	Our families quite ruin'd.
Lord Lacy	Take courage, gentlemen. Comfort may appear,
	And punishment overtake him when he least expects it.

Exeunt

ACT 5, SCENE 3

[*A table, chair and wine set out.*] PLENTY *ready to speak within*

Enter Sir John [FRUGAL, *as an Indian*,] *and* HOLDFAST

Frugal	Be silent, on your life.
Holdfast	I am o'erjoy'd.
Frugal	Are the pictures plac'd as I directed?
Holdfast	Yes, sir.
Frugal	And the musicians ready?
Holdfast	All is done
	As you commanded.
Frugal	Make haste, and be careful.
	[*At the door*] You know your cue and postures?
Plenty	[*within*] We are perfect.
Frugal	'Tis well. [*To* HOLDFAST] The rest are come too?

Holdfast	And dispos'd of
	To your own wish.
Frugal	Set forth the table. So.

Enter servants with a rich banquet

A perfect banquet. At the upper end,
His chair in state; he shall feast like a prince.

Holdfast   And rise like a Dutch hangman.

Enter LUKE

Frugal   Not a word more.   10
[*To* LUKE] How like you the preparation? Fill your room
And taste the cates; then in your thought consider
A rich man that lives wisely to himself
In his full height of glory.

Luke   I can brook
No rival in this happiness. How sweetly
These dainties, when unpaid for, please my palate!
Some wine, Jove's nectar! Brightness to the star
That govern'd at my birth. Shoot down thy influence,
And with a perpetuity of being,
Continue this felicity, not gain'd   20
By vows to saints above, and much less purchas'd
By thriving industry, nor fall'n upon me
As a reward to piety and religion
Or service for my country. I owe all this
To dissimulation and the shape
I wore of goodness. Let my brother number
His beads devoutly and believe his alms
To beggars, his compassion to his debtors,
Will wing his better part, disrob'd of flesh,
To soar above the firmament. I am well,   30

	And so I surfeit here in all abundance.	
	Though styl'd a cormorant, a cut-throat, Jew,	
	And prosecuted with the fatal curses	
	Of widows, undone orphans and what else	
	Such as malign my state can load me with,	
	I will not envy it. [*To* FRUGAL] You promis'd music?	
Frugal	And you shall hear the strength and power	
	Of it, the spirit of Orpheus rais'd to make it good,	
	And in those ravishing strains with which he mov'd	
	Charon and Cerberus to give him way	40
	To fetch from hell his lost Eurydice.	
	[*To players*] Appear swifter than thought.	

Music. At one door, Cerberus; *at the other,* Charon, Orpheus, Chorus.
[*They mime the story of Orpheus in the Underworld. Exeunt*]

Luke	'Tis wondrous strange.
Frugal	Does not the object and the accent take you?

PLENTY *and* [Sir Maurice] LACY *ready behind*

Luke	A pretty fable. But that music should
	Alter in fiends their nature is to me
	Impossible, since in myself I find
	What I have once decreed shall know no change.
Frugal	You are constant to your purposes, yet I think
	That I could stagger you.
Luke	How?
Frugal	Should I present
	Your servants, debtors and the rest that suffer 50
	By your fit severity, I presume the sight
	Would move you to compassion.
Luke	Not a mote.

The music that your Orpheus made was harsh
To the delight I should receive in hearing
Their cries and groans. If it be in your power,
I would now see 'em.

Frugal   Spirits in their shapes
Shall show them as they are. But if it should move you?

Luke   If it do, may I ne'er find pity.

Frugal   Be your own judge.
[*To 'apparitions' offstage*] Appear as I commanded!

Sad music. Enter [Young] GOLDWIRE *and* [Young] TRADEWELL
as from prison, FORTUNE, HOIST [*and*] PENURY *following after them,*
SHAVE'EM *in a blue gown,* SECRET, DING'EM, OLD
TRADEWELL, *and* OLD GOLDWIRE *with* SERGEANTS.
As directed, they all kneel to LUKE, *heaving up their hands for mercy.*
[*Enter*] STARGAZE *with a pack of almanacs,* [*and*] MILLICENT

Luke   Ha, ha, ha!
This move me to compassion? Or raise   60
One sign of seeming pity in my face?
You are deceiv'd. It rather renders me
More flinty and obdurate. A south wind
Shall sooner soften marble, and the rain
That slides down gently from his flaggy wings
O'erflow the Alps, than knees or tears or groans
Shall wrest compunction from me. 'Tis my glory
That they are wretched, and by me made so.
It sets my happiness off. I could not triumph
If these were not my captives. Ha! My terriers,   70
As it appears, have seiz'd on these old foxes,
As I gave order. New addition to
My scene of mirth. Ha, ha! They now grow tedious.

Let 'em be remov'd.

[*Exeunt* Young GOLDWIRE, Young TRADEWELL, FORTUNE,
     HOIST, PENURY, SHAVE'EM, SECRET, DING'EM,
OLD TRADEWELL, OLD GOLDWIRE, SERGEANTS,
          STARGAZE *and* MILLICENT]
                              Some other object, if
Your art can show it.

Frugal   You shall perceive 'tis boundless.
               Yet one thing real, if you please?

Luke   What is it?

Frugal   Your nieces ere they put to sea, crave humbly –
              Though absent in their bodies – they may take leave
              Of their late suitors' statues.

          Enter LADY [FRUGAL], ANNE *and* MARY;
          [*portraits of* Sir Maurice LACY *and* PLENTY *discovered aloft*]

Luke   There they hang.
              In things indifferent I am tractable.   80

Frugal   There pay your vows; you have liberty.

Anne   [*to Lacy's portrait*]   O, sweet figure
              Of my abused Lacy! When remov'd
              Into another world, I'll daily pay
              A sacrifice of sighs to thy remembrance,
              And with a shower of tears strive to wash off
              The stain of that contempt my foolish pride
              And insolence threw upon thee.

Mary   [*to Plenty's portrait*]   I had been
              Too happy if I had enjoy'd the substance,
              But far unworthy of it; now I shall
              Thus prostrate to thy statue.

Lady Frugal	My kind husband, 90

Blessed in my misery, from the monastery
To which my disobedience confin'd thee,
With thy soul's eye – which distance cannot hinder –
Look on my penitence. Oh, that I could
Call back time past, thy holy vow dispens'd,
With what humility would I observe
My long neglected duty.

Frugal   Does not this move you?

Luke   Yes, as they do the statues, and her sorrow
My absent brother. If by your magic art
You can give life to these, or bring him hither   100
To witness her repentence, I may have
(Perchance) some feeling of it.

Frugal   For your sport
You shall see a masterpiece. Here's nothing but
A superficies – colours and no substance.
Sit still, and to your wonder and amazement
I'll give these organs. This the sacrifice
To make the great work perfect.
          [Sir John FRUGAL *feigns magic*; *the portraits of*
Sir Maurice, LACY *and* PLENTY *show signs of animation*]

Luke   Prodigious!

Frugal   Nay, they have life and motion. Descend.
                    [Sir Maurice LACY *and* PLENTY *step from behind*
                              their portraits and descend to the main stage]
And for your absent brother, this wash'd off,
Against your will you shall know him.
          [*Removes his disguise.* LADY FRUGAL, ANNE *and* MARY *kneel*]

          Enter LORD LACY *and the rest*

Luke	I am lost. 110
	Guilt strikes me dumb.
Frugal	[*to* LORD LACY] You have seen, my lord, the pageant?
Lord Lacy	I have, and am ravish'd with it.
Frugal	What think you now
	Of this clear soul, this honest pious man?
	Have I stripp'd him bare? Or will your lordship
	Have a farther trial of him? 'Tis not in
	A wolf to change his nature.
Lord Lacy	I have long since
	Confess'd my error.
Frugal	[*to* LADY FRUGAL, ANNE *and* MARY] Look up,
	I forgive you,
	And seal your pardon thus.

> [FRUGAL *raises and embraces* LADY FRUGAL,
> ANNE *and* MARY]

Lady Frugal	I am too full
	Of joy to speak it.
Anne	I am another creature,
	Not what I was.
Mary	I vow to show myself, 120
	When I am married, an humble wife,
	Not a commanding mistress.
Plenty	[*to* MARY] On those terms
	I gladly thus embrace you. [*They embrace*]
Lacy	[*to* ANNE] Welcome to
	My bosom. As the one half of myself,
	I'll love you and cherish you. [*They embrace*]

Goldwire	[*to* Sir John FRUGAL]	Mercy!

Tradewell   Good sir, mercy!
and the rest

Frugal   This day is sacred to it. All shall find me,
                As far as lawful pity can give way to't,
                Indulgent to your wishes, though with loss
                Unto myself. My kind and honest brother,
                Looking into yourself, have you seen the gorgon?   130
                What a golden dream you have had in the possession
                Of my estate! But here's a revocation
                That wakes you out of it – monster in nature,
                Revengeful, avaricious atheist,
                Transcending all example. But shall I be
                A sharer in thy crimes? Should I repeat 'em?
                What wilt thou do? Turn hypocrite again,
                With hope dissimulation can aid thee?
                Or that one eye will shed a tear in sign
                Of sorrow for thee? I have warrant to   140
                Make bold with mine own. Pray you, uncase. This key, too,
                I must make bold with. Hide thyself in some desert
                Where good men ne'er may find thee, or in justice
                Pack to Virginia and repent, not for
                Those horrid ends to which thou did'st design these.

Luke   I care not where I go. What's done with words
                Cannot be undone.   *Exit* LUKE

Lady Frugal   Yet, sir, show some mercy
                Because his cruelty to me and mine
                Did good upon us.

Frugal   Of that, at better leisure,
                As his penitency shall work me. Make you good   150
                Your promis'd reformation, and instruct

Our city dames (whom wealth makes proud) to move
In their own spheres and willingly to confess
In their habits, manners and their highest port
A distance 'twixt the city and the court.   *Exeunt omnes*

FINIS

ACKNOWLEDGEMENTS

Thanks to all those whose help contributed to this edition of Massinger's *The City Madam*, especially previous editors for their useful commentaries on the play, and to the British Library for permission to reprint the first text page from one of their copies of the first quarto (C.123.d.9). Gordon McMullan patiently answered my endless questions and read drafts with a thorough and scholarly eye; Gabriel Egan provided invaluable technical help; Tom Berger took over as general editor in the final stages, making many useful suggestions and corrections; and Phil Withington displayed his usual good humour in the face of my obsessions. This book is dedicated to my parents, Alan and Lucy Shrank, who will appreciate a play about high-handed madams who get their come-uppance.

Cathy Shrank
Editor

GLOSSARIAL NOTES

DRAMATIS PERSONAE

19	*wench*	prostitute
20	*hectors*	insolent fellows, braggarts
23	*box-keeper*	keeper of dice and box at a gaming table

DEDICATORY EPISTLE

2   *Lady Ann*   Ann de Vere (d. 1659), first wife of Aubrey de Vere, 20th earl of Oxford. There are two variant editions of the first quarto of *The City Madam*: those dated 1659 are all dedicated to Lady Ann de Vere, Countess of Oxford; those dated 1658 are dedicated to various addressees (namely Lady Ann, John Wrath, Thomas Freake, Richard Steadwell and Mr Lee), presumably to allow Pennyquick to approach a range of potential patrons. In each case, the dedicatory epistle is the same, save for the requisite alterations to the heading, address and subscription

15   *many*   many plays

24   *Andrew Pennycuick*   one of the original actors in *The City Madam*

1.1

1   *the Pool*   part of the River Thames between London Bridge and Limehouse

4-5   *hundred ... five*   Frugal has made a five-fold profit on his investment

6   *on the nail*   immediately

9   *addition*   title added to a name to show respect

11   scandalum magnatum   'utterance of a malicious report against a person of dignity' (*OED*)

24   *bravery*   ostentation

26   *masque*   amateur dramatic entertainment, containing singing and dancing, popular at court in the first half of the seventeenth century

27   *habits*   clothes

32	*for Sir John* instead of Sir John
35	*the Counter* name of two debtors' prisons in seventeenth-century London (one at Wood Street, the other at the Poultry)
36	*the hole* where prisoners in the Counter, who were unable to pay for better accommodation in the prison, were obliged to reside (i.e. the worst place in the Counter)
40	*beneath the salt* the salt-cellar was traditionally placed in the middle of the table; people of superior rank sat above it, those of inferior rank, below
43	*under-prentice* junior apprentice
52	*wagtails* 'contemptuous epithet applied to a young man or woman' (*OED* 3a)
58	*parts* office, duties
59-60	*curious … nativities* studious in casting the horoscopes
62	*curiosity* determination
64	*church-book* church records, which would show the date of baptism
67	*humour* temperament
72-7	*As … justice* Millicent here shows an extraordinary degree of upwardly-mobile ambition, both for her mistress and herself
73	*walk bare* take his hat off in her presence (a sign of respect)
76	*take the upper hand* take precedence
77	*justice* justice of the peace (referring to the squire, over whose wife Millicent hopes to take precedence)
97	*skins* leather
98	*prison-bird* Luke (referring to the time he spent in debtors' prison)
104.5	SD] *roses* ornamental knots of ribbon (shaped like a rose) to be worn on the fronts of shoes
	like hen, like chicken like mother, like daughter
106	*frippery* place where cast-off clothes were sold
110	*sirrah* term of address to men or boys used to express contempt and/or the superiority of the speaker
113	*patrimony* property inherited from father
114	*sheriff's basket* 'basket or tub placed outside a prison to receive charitable doles for the prisoners' (*OED* 4b)
	broken meat 'fragments of food left after a meal' (*OED* 1b)

115   *festival exceedings*   extra allowance of food for special occasions
123   *beggar's satisfaction*   beggar's payment (without money, the beggar
      can only repay a debt with prayers)
128   *the Old Exchange*   exchange: building in a city or town where
      merchants assembled to do business; the Old Exchange, the
      original London exchange, formerly the Royal Exchange (from
      1570), termed the Old Exchange after the building of a second
      exchange in 1609
131   *breathe*   put out of breath, exhaust
      footman   foot-servant who would run alongside his master's horse
140   *perfume ... in*   Millicent is referring to the effect of Lady
      Frugal's shoes of perfumed leather
      fur   'to put under her feet while he tried on her shoes' (John
      Monck Mason, ed., *Dramatick Works of Philip Massinger*, vol. 4,
      1779)
147   *roots*   root vegetables (e.g. carrots and turnips)
149   *go down*   be swallowed
152   *Fleet Lane and Pie Corner*   streets in the City of London which
      proliferated in cooks' shops
157   *want*   lack, miss
157-8 *you ... ends*   Holdfast is here suggesting the French and Italian
      cooks will steal the silver

1.2

3   *gallant*   man of fashion
      latest edition   latest fashion
7   *caution*   word of warning (*OED* 3)
9-10 *until ... choice*   Lacy has not yet decided which of the two
      daughters he will marry; since it is primarily Frugal's wealth that
      makes the match attractive, the relative charms of either daughter
      are of secondary consideration (cf. Mary, 2.1.77-8)
14   *though ... his*   as though Lacy had already succeeded to the title (of
      lord) he will inherit on his father's death
      reversion   'right of succeeding to, or next occupying, an estate'
      (*OED* 1b)

15   *freeman* one who possesses the freedom of a city or borough
16   *in ... affection* in matters of love
18   *sat ... porter* acted as gate-keeper
20   *piece* piece of money, coin, given here as a tip
23   *institution* instruction
25   *seal ... duellist* enter into a duel
28   *big* haughty
28-9   *loose ... breadth* remove my hat (as a sign of respect)
29   *beaver* hat made of beaver's fur
30   *prove* test
32   *breathe* excercise
        Moorfields piece of open ground north of the old city wall
33   *Toledo* sword made in Toledo, Spain
35   *clubs* used by London apprentices to break up disturbances of the
        peace; 'Clubs' was the rallying cry for apprentices to summon help in a
        brawl
37   *hinds* household servants
43   *gay* 'sportive, merry' (*OED* 1)
46   *your* used here as an indefinite article, a form that often expresses
        contempt (*OED* 5b)
48   *incident* natural
52   *paid brokage ... scrivener* bribed the usurer's clerk (to falsify the amount
        owed)
53   *mercer* dealer in silks, velvets and other expensive materials
54   *peascods* pea-pods
57   *Smithfield* London meat-market
58   *jointure* 'holding of property to the joint use of a husband and
        wife for life or in tail, as a provision for the latter, in the event of her
        widowhood. Hence, by extension, a sole estate limited to the wife'
        (*OED* 4a, b)
59   *encumber'd* burdened with debt
        annuity yearly allowance; in this case, meaning a yearly allowance paid
        out of rents on the property to someone other than the owner
65   *Stoics* followers of the classical Greek school of philosophy
        characterised for its austerity; by extension, those indifferent to pain or
        pleasure

68	*grazier* someone who feeds cattle for the market
69	*hundred* 'sub-division of a county or shire, having its own court; also applied to the court itself' (*OED* 5a)
71	*threshers* henchmen
74	*bum-blades* large swords
75	*house* plunge the blade into the body (a sword would usually be housed in a scabbard)
79	*fame* reputation
87	*next* nearest
93	*argument* subject of contention
94	*salute* i.e. greet Frugal's daughters
98	*make ... approaches* make advances, i.e. court Frugal's daughters
103	SD] *omnes praeter* all except
113	*cocking* cock-fighting
118	*pitch* 'height to which a falcon or other bird of prey soars before swooping down on its prey' (*OED* 18a)
133	*long* long-lived
143	*wear scarlet* attain civic office, e.g. become an alderman or lord mayor (referring to the colour of their ceremonial robes)
146	*carriage* behaviour

1.3

SD]	*standish* 'a stand containing ink, pens and other writing materials and accessories' (*OED*)
3	*call in* reclaim the money owed
5.5	SD] *placing the Lord Lacy* positioning him where he can observe the scene that follows, whilst remaining unobserved himself
7	*ordinaries* 'public meal provided at a fixed price in an eating house or tavern; also, the company frequenting such a meal' (*OED* 14a)
8	*livery punk* prostitute kept for the use of the client for a fixed price
9	*money-monger* dealer in money, especially in lending it
10	*longer day* more time
19	*infidel* unbeliever; from a Christian point of view, someone who does not hold with the tenets of Christianity (here, honouring your duty to provide for your family)

21-2   *An ... man*   sufficient amount to live on for a reputable man
28   *Ludgate*   name of a debtors' prison in London, 'anciently appropriated
        to the freemen of the city', one of the best endowed and governed
        prisons in London (W. Gifford, ed. *Plays of Philip Massinger*, vol. 4,
        1805)
38   *protest*   'to make a formal written declaration of the non-acceptance or
        non-payment of (a bill of exchange) when duly present' (Hoy, ed., *City
        Madam*)
54-5   *flies ... high*   is equally esteemed
71   *beasts of rapine*   beasts of prey
76   *outcry*   public auction
82   *brave*   intrepid (*OED* 1), grand (*OED* 2), worthy (*OED* 3); the
        multiple senses of the word capture both the risks taken, the wealth
        displayed, and the consequent high reputation of the merchant
        Fortune in his prime
83   *decay'd*   impoverished
89   *nor ... wealth*   this is spoken to Plenty
96   *divines*   theologians
97   *effectually*   pertinently
101   *beadsmen*   men who pray for the soul or spiritual welfare of another
102   *next*   after (i.e. their first thanks will be to God, then to Frugal)
117   *break*   break the bargain; fail to meet their obligations and repay the
        debt
118   *orator*   advocate or spokesperson who speaks on behalf of a person or
        cause
119   *Counter*   see above 1.1.35n
123   *all of a piece*   consistent
132   *parasite*   'one who eats at the table or at the expense of another; always
        with opprobrious application' (*OED* 1a)
136   *take me with you*   hear me out
159   *in the touch*   'action of testing the quality of gold and silver by rubbing
        it on a touchstone' (*OED* 5a)

2.1

4	*ambergris* 'wax-like substance of marbled ashy colour, found floating in tropical seas, and as a morbid secretion in the intestines of the sperm-whale. It is odoriferous and used in perfumery; formerly in cookery' (*OED*); included here as an exotic and expensive substance
5	*wethers* castrated rams
	bruis'd pounded, ground
9	*sucking pigs* young milk-fed pigs suitable for roasting whole
10	*took … farrow'd* taken from the mother as soon as she has produced the litter
11	*muscadine* 'strong sweet wine made from the Muscat, or similar, grape' (*OED*)
12	*marks* coins worth 13 shillings and 4 old pence each, two-thirds of a pound sterling
13	*puddings* stomachs of pigs, sheep, or other animals, stuffed with a mixture of minced meat, suet, oatmeal and seasoning, and then boiled
15	*Dutchman* German, stereotyped in the period for excessive eating and drinking
19	*woodmongers* timber-merchants
	billets wood cut for fuel
22	*banquet* course of sweetmeats, fruit and wine, often served in another room after the main meal
27	*give up his cloak* resign (the cloak being a symbol of office)
30	*Great Fiend* Satan
44	*indentures* 'contract by which an apprentice is bound to the master who undertakes to teach him a trade' (*OED* 2b)
46	*other world* the East Indies
51	*tincture* trace
52	*mechanics* 'having a manual occupation' (*OED* 2)
63	*Counter* see above 1.1.35n
67	*cautelous* crafty, cautious
71	*cloth of bodkin* richly embroidered material, brocade, or shot silk
73	*gross* total
81	*ordinary* 'eating-house or tavern where public meals are provided at a fixed price; a dining-room in such a building' (*OED* 14b)
	cap-a-pie from head to foot

82   *trunks … furnish'd* the apprentices will have to keep their finery hidden while they are in Frugal's house
87   *braveries* gallants
88   *occurrents* news
90   *censure* pass judgement on
95   *fill his room* take his place
96   *fellows* equals
98   *lucky hand* winning hand of cards
99   *buy out your time* pay to reduce the time of the apprenticeship remaining
102   *madam-punk* prostitute
103   *cambric* fine white linen
108   *Brentford* town in Middlesex, eight miles west of London
        Staines town in Middlesex, seventeen miles west of London
        Barnet town in Hertfordshire, eleven miles northwest of London; these three towns, lying outside the jurisdiction of the city, were associated with illicit sex
110   *pagans* prostitutes
113   *'The shaking of the sheets'* tune, also referring to sexual intercourse
114   *cockatrice* prostitute
122   *correspondence* communication
127   *Ka me, ka thee* help me and I'll help you
        knot bond
131   *cater* buyer of provisions within a household
132   *Barbican* street north-west of Moorgate
        outside outer garments
133   *crash* bout of revelry
        ordinary see above, 2.1.81n
135   *proper* own
136   *What did you make me?* referring to the fact that Young Goldwire has made Luke a pander or go-between
138   *excuse* make an excuse for
141   *end* intention

2.2

4	*entail* 'settle land, estate, etc. on a number of persons in succession, so that it cannot be bequeathed at pleasure by any one possessor' (*OED* 1)
19	*consult of* discuss
22	*copy* 'copyhold (tenure of lands that were part of a manor was said to be "by copy," i.e., according to the copy of the manorial court-roll)' (Hoy, ed., *City Madam*)
24	*business ... talk'd of* Frugal is here referring to their previous discussion about Luke
29	*schemes* 'diagram showing the relative positions of the heavenly bodies' (*OED* 2a)
33	*parcel* part
35	*potatoes* sweet potatoes, 'supposed in the sixteenth and seventeenth centuries to have aphrodisiac qualities' (*OED* 1a)
36	*encomiums* 'formal or high-blown expression of praise' (*OED*)
37	*antecedent* someone who walks in front (a sign of the rank of the person who follows)
42	*judicial astrology* now called astrology
43	*penny almanac* cheap calendar with astronomical data and calculations and other useful information
48	*latitude* region (defined by the latitude – ie. the distance north or south of the equator – on which it lies)
49	SD] *schemes* see above, 2.2.29n
51	*articulate* 'arrange by articles or conditions' (*OED* 9), referring here to the marriage contracts
54-5	*in omni/Parte, et toto* in every part and the whole
57	*pleasant* facetious
58	*vulgar tongue* the vernacular (i.e. English); 'vulgar' here is not denigratory
60-85	Stargaze's predictions are phrased in deliberately pretentious and obscure language, signalling his own status as a fraud
60	*trine* 'denoting the 'aspect' of two heavenly bodies which are a third part of the zodiac, i.e. 120°, distant from each other' (*OED* 2)
	conjunction 'apparent proximity of two planets or other heavenly bodies' (*OED* 3)

61   *almuten* 'prevailing or ruling planet in the horoscope' (*OED*)
62   *Hoyday!* exclamation of surprise
63   *geniture* synonym for horoscope
64   *reception* 'fact of each of two planets being received into the other's
        house, exaltation, or other dignity' (*OED* 2a)
64   *exaltation* 'place of a planet in the zodiac in which it was considered to
        exert its greatest influence' (*OED* 3)
65   *triplicity* 'combination of three of the twelve signs of the zodiac, each
        sign being distant 120° or the third part of a circle from the other two'
        (*OED* 3)
        trine see above 2.2.60n
        face 'third part of a sign of the zodiac, extending over 10 degrees in
        longitude' (*OED* 11c)
66   *Hymen* Roman god of marriage
75   *dignities* 'situation of a planet in which its influence is heightened,
        either by its position in the zodiac, or by its aspects with other planets'
        (*OED* 5)
76   *detriment* 'position or condition of a planet when in the sign opposite
        its house; a condition of weakness or distress' (*OED* 2)
        combust when planets are seemingly extinguished by the sun's light
        when in near conjunction with the sun
78   *occidental* west
79   *oriental* east
79-80   *in* cazimi 'when a planet is distant not more than seventeen minutes,
        or half its apparent diameter, from the sun' (*OED*)
81   *infortunes* misfortunes
83   *radix* 'basis of calculation, as a nativity, a certain point in time,
        position of a planet' (*OED* 1)
88   *Chaldeans* 'native of Chaldea, especially (as at Babylon) one skilled in
        occult learning, astrology, etc.; hence in general, a seer, soothsayer,
        astrologer' (*OED*)
        Zoroastes legendary Persian prophet (also called Zarathustra),
        traditionally born 628 BCE, connected with occult and magical
        practices
89   *Mercurius Trismegistus* 'thrice greatest Hermes', 'name given by Neo-
        Platonists and the devotees of mysticism and alchemy to the Egyptian

god Thoth, regarded as the author of all mysterious doctrines, and especially the secrets of alchemy' (*OED*)

the later Ptolemy Alexandrian astronomer, active 121-151 CE

90   *prognosticator* soothsayer

90   *Erra Pater* 'said to have been the name of an ancient Jewish astrologer' (E. Cobham Brewer, *Dictionary of Phrase and Fable*, 1898); the name also sounds like 'father of error' (from the Latin *pater*)

101   *van* vanguard, i.e comes in front (referring to Anne's precedence, as the elder sister)

107   imprimis in the first place

108   *one* i.e. a lady

111   *caroche* luxurious seventeenth-century coach

113   *postilion* 'one who rides the near horse of the leaders when four or more are used in a carriage or post-chaise' (*OED* 3)

121   *that sit on the stage* gallants would pay to sit and watch plays from stools on the stage, where their often-distracting behaviour irritated players and playwrights (Andrew Gurr, *The Shakespearean Stage*, 3rd edn, 1992)

130-2   *may ... throat* proverbial; cf. 'The Devil run through you booted and spurred with a scythe on his back' (Morris Palmer Tilley, *A Dictionary of Proverbs in England in the Sixteenth and Seventeenth Centuries*, 1950)

137   *exordium* beginning

143   *she ... close* she upholds her principles firmly

148   *stone* measure of weight

149   *bring in* produce

bring ... butter Mary is here possibly mocking the frugality of the country-wife she disdains

151   *cut* castrate

capons castrated cockerels

against in preparation for

155   *eye your threshers* keep an eye on Plenty's harvesters, to ensure they are working; also has sexual undertones, of Mary lusting after the workmen

158   *clowns* countrymen

164   *state* estate

165   *he* her husband

166   *viragos* female warriors, manly women

171   *owes* owns
181   *sparhawk* sparrowhawk
183   *stand on* take a stand on (i.e. cause difficulties about)
186   *Like bitch, like whelps* like mother, like daughter; cf. 1.1.104
187   *House of Pride* depicted in Spenser's *Faerie Queene* (1590), Book I, canto 6
189   *morris* morris-dance; the 'lady' in a morris dance is a female fool; see
       Shakespeare and Fletcher's *Two Noble Kinsmen* (1613), 3.5
190   *punk, trull* strumpet, prostitute
192   *Jacob's staff* instrument using for measuring the altitude of the sun
197   *sow-gelder* someone who spays sows
198   *lib* castrate
200   *worried* killed or injured by biting and shaking (how many dogs kill
       their prey), here responding to the preceding reference to bear-baiting
202   *only this* Lacy characteristically insists that he will refrain from hurling
       insults, before proceeding to produce them; cf. his words to Plenty,
       1.2.67.
       peats 'term of endearment used to a girl or woman = pet of a woman;
       hence with various shades of meaning = girl simply, light or merry
       girl, fondled or spoilt girl, etc.' (*OED* 1); here, used contemptuously
207   *lead apes in hell* proverbial occupation of spinsters in the afterlife
209   *juggler* 'one who plays tricks by sleight of hand' (*OED* 2)
212   *astrolabe* 'instrument used to take altitudes, and to solve other
       problems of practical astronomy' (*OED*)
221   *mettle* temperament (*OED* 1)

                                  2.3

1   *plot* to reveal Luke in his true colours
13   *north passage* the discovery of a northerly route to the East was a
       preoccupation of seventeenth-century maritime explorers
15   *Proserpine* (or Persephone) wife of Pluto, Roman god of the
       Underworld
17   *Cerberus* three-headed dog guarding the entrance to the Underworld
       furies three avenging goddesses of classical mythology, sent from the
       Underworld to punish crime

26   *same leaven* out of the same batch of bread, i.e. of the same nature
28   *upon record* evidence in writing that may be appealed to in case of
      dispute (*OED* 1)
30   *articl'd* set out particular conditions
31   *aforehand* before (in this case, before marriage)
40   *licence* permission
49   *abroad* outside

3.1

1   *doings* sexual intercourse ('dead doings' referring to the fact that
      Shave'em is getting little custom)
4.5   SD] music[ians] come down the musicians come down from the
      gallery, ready to enter at 3.1.55
5   *striker* fornicator
13   *Burse* the New Exchange (as opposed to the Old Exchange, see
      1.1.128)
14   *neathouse* literally, a shed in which cattle were kept; here refers to an
      area near Chelsea Bridge where there was a famous market-garden
15   *asparagus* reputed as an aphrodisiac because of its phallic shape
18   *dancing of the ropes* rope-dancing; Shave'em infers that Secret is
      suggesting she look for customers in the playhouses (a notorious haunt
      of prostitutes), where the rope-dancers would perform
19   *nuts and pippins* nuts and apples (pippins) which were sold at the
      playhouses
20   *chapman* merchant, trader
22   *drum-wine* wine sold publicly ('by the drum', *OED* 1c)
24   *sisterhood* of prostitutes
26   *Clarissimi* highest ranking members of Venetian society
27   *hot-rein'd* lecherous, reins being 'the region of the kidneys; the loins'
      (*OED*)
      marmoset small monkey, renowned to be lecherous; also used to mean
      'favourite, ingle' (*OED* 3b)
28   *their country's honour* the French and Italians were stereotypically
      lecherous

28/29   *vacation/term*   parodying the terminology of the Inns of Court; just as, after the vacation, lawyers return for business during the law terms, so too the ambassadors' retinues will signal the prostitute's return to the business of sexual intercourse after an enforced vacation from it, during the slack period of trade about which Shave'em and Secret complain at the beginning of this scene

33   *suburbian*   suburban

    roarers   'noisy, riotous bully' (*OED* 1b)

34   *truckers*   hagglers

38   *close ward*   near the defences

43   *waistcoateer*   low-class prostitute

46   *spital*   charitable foundation for receiving the indigent or diseased

50   *brach*   bitch

51   *turn'd mankind*   become mannish

57   *I can but ride*   be carted (carried in a cart), a punishment for whoring

58   *Paul's*   Paul's Cross, outside St Paul's, where sermons were preached

    smok'd   smoked out, exposed

60   *Romford*   town in Essex, twelve miles northeast of London

72   *lavolta*   'lively dance for two persons, consisting a good deal in high and active bounds' (*OED*, quoting Robert Nares, *A Glossary*, 1822)

73   *device*   invention

74   *pig-sconce*   pig-head

83   *cashier'd*   dismissed from a position of authority

84   *entertainment*   wages

91   *furnish'd*   with money

93   *appurtenances*   accessories

96   *pantables*   slippers (variant of pantofles)

97   *banquet*   see above, 2.1.22n.

    caudle   warm drink of thin gruel mixed with wine or ale, sweetened and spiced

98   *against*   for when

3.2

1   *beadsman*   almsman, someone dependent on charity in return for their prayers on behalf of their benefactor(s); cf. 1.3.101

10   *discourse* faculty of reason
20   *paternoster* Latin for 'Our Father', the Lord's Prayer; the use of the
        Latin form of the prayer suggests Catholicism
26   *eyes clos'd* i.e. dead
29-30   *I ... do* Lady Frugal knows Luke is eloquent, but she wants him to
        produce more than fine speeches: she wants him to do what he says
34   *Master Frugal* Sir John Frugal (a slip symptomatic of the text's
        confusion regarding names; see 'Editor's Introduction', p. xi)
55-6   *wind ... fair* wind being in a favourable direction and of suitable
        strength (i.e. neither a calm nor too stormy) to ensure a swift and easy
        journey by boat to the French coast
57   *Louvain* university town in what is now Belgium; location of one of
        the key seminaries despatching Jesuit priests to England, and a place of
        refuge for many English Catholics
78   *decay'd* see above, 1.3.83n
79   *coagent* i.e. Frugal and his wife have acted together in their harshness
        towards Luke
86   *movables* personal property (property that can be moved, as opposed to
        landed property)
90   *groat* small denomination coin worth four old pence
131   *jubilee ... joy* tautological, since jubilee means, in this context, 'a
        season or occasion of joyful celebration' (*OED* 4)
138   *principal* original sum lent
146   *fit* proper, appropriate
155-6   *wide ... region* very mistaken
164   *Juno* queen of the Roman gods; wife of Jupiter, king of the gods
165   *Iris* Roman goddess of the rainbow, who acted as messenger of the
        gods
        Hebe one of the daughters of Juno and Jupiter, goddess of youth and
        spring and cup-bearer to the gods
169   *Hermes* messenger of the gods in Greek mythology (Roman
        equivalent, Mercury), symbolised by his winged sandals and caduceus
        (see below, 170)
170   *caduceus* staff carried by Hermes or Mercury, usually depicted with
        two serpents wrapped around it
198   *go no less* I'll not play for a smaller stake (gambling phrase)

199   *night-rail* dressing-gown

3.3

11   *Hermes' moly* herb given to Odysseus (or Ulysses) by Hermes to protect him against the sorceress Circe (Homer, *Odyssey*, X)

12   *Sibylla's golden bough* taken by Aeneas, on the instructions of the Sibyl of Cumae, as an offering to Persephone (or Proserpine) when he descended to the Underworld (Vergil, *Aeneid*, VI)
       great elixir believed to turn base metals into gold

18   *by-corners* out-of-the-way corners

36   *manor ... parchment* referring to the deeds granting the right of ownership of the manor (here given as surety for a loan)

38   *deed of gift* legal document recognising a bequest from one party to another (again, here given as surety for a loan)

40   *unthrift* someone who is financially imprudent

43   *sublim'd* exalted

45.5   SD] *Indians* indigenous peoples of North America

74   *Virginia* earliest British colony in North America (the first settlement dating from 1607)

92-4   *Oh, ha ... bonnery* Frugal, Lacy and Plenty invent an 'Indian'-sounding language

96   *doctors* theological doctors, divines

108   *Plutus* Roman god of wealth

4.1

3   *quondam* former
       ingles favourites, catamites, bosom friends

8   *don* Spanish title, prefixed to Christian name, showing high rank or used as a courtesy

9   *Bridewell* house of correction, particularly for prostitutes
       the hole see above 1.1.36n
       comrogues fellow rogues

16   *scrape-shoe* obsequious person

22   *golls* hands

24   *factor* agent
25   *Helen* Helen of Troy, i.e. a beautiful (if promiscuous) woman, here
      referring to Shave'em
28   *Paris* Helen of Troy's lover, who stole her from her husband
      Menelaus, causing the Trojan War
36   *myriad* literally, ten thousand
39   *but* except
42   *box* referring to Getall's position as box-keeper (see above, *Dramatis
      Personae*)
45   *pontifical* popish, having the dignity and pomp of a pope
50   *Old Aeson* father of the mythological hero, Jason, who was
      rejuvenated by Medea's magic
51   *Medea* sorceress from the island of Colchis, who helped Jason obtain
      the golden fleece; see above 4.1.50n
      restoratives potions that will bring back lost youth (see above, 4.1.50n),
      here referring to the cosmetics Shave'em will use to make herself look
      younger
71   *cap ... sword* symbols of office, borne before the Lord Mayor
73   *Burse* see above, 3.1.13n
75   *Gresham* Thomas Gresham (1519?-1579), founder of the Royal (or
      Old) Exchange and one of London's most famous early modern
      citizens
75-6 *conduits ... sack* on festival occasions, such as the inauguration of the
      Lord Mayor or a royal entry to the city, the conduits – or water
      fountains – in London would be made to run with wine (Canary sack
      being a type of sweet white wine imported from the Canary Islands)
76-7 *not ... pounds* all the prisoners whose debts amount to less than £10
      having been released (through Luke's benevolence)
90   *Barbary* north coast of Africa
91   *Gravesend* port on the Thames in Kent
92   *find* 'receive advantage from' (*OED* 4a)
95   *execution* 'process under which the sheriff or other officer is
      commanded to execute a judgement' (*OED* 7), in this case, to press for
      the immediate repayment of the loan
99   *competence* sufficient means to live comfortably
102   *three days' patience* three days' grace before payment is required

106   *good husband*   man who manages their affairs with prudence and thrift

4.2

4   *'At all!'*   gambler's call to signify they will play for any sum anyone
        chooses to wager (*Monthly Mirror*, January 1807, cited by Cyrus Hoy,
        ed., *City Madam*, 1964)
7   *habiliments* ' apparel, vestments, or garments appropriate to any office
        or occasion. Applied also, jocularly or grandiloquently, to ordinary
        clothes' (*OED* 4)
10   *drabber*   frequenter of prostitutes
14   *oil of talc*   'preparation used as a cosmetic' (*OED* 1)
15   *ceruses*   white lead, used as cosmetic
25   *Cheapside*   one of the main city thoroughfares and where the
        goldsmiths traditionally had their shops
27   *St Martin's*   site of St Martin's-le-Grand, destroyed at the dissolution
        of the monasteries in 1530s; the privileges of sanctuary remained,
        however, and the area became a refuge for criminals and debtors
        avoiding arrest
        procurer   bawd (i.e. Secret)
32   *consort*   company of musicians
33   *Comus*   personification of revelry
39   *Cleopatra*   legendarily seductive ruler of Egypt in 1st century BCE,
        lover of Julius Caesar and Mark Antony (see below, 4.2.41)
41   *Antony*   the Roman general Mark Antony, Cleopatra's last lover,
        renowned for his extravagence
        nine worthies   nine famous men of ancient and medieval history and
        legend (namely, Joshua, David, Judas Maccabæus, Hector, Alexander,
        Julius Cæsar, King Arthur, Charlemagne and Godfrey of Bouillon)
51   *Venus*   Roman goddess of love
67   *ware the caster*   'when a setter supposes himself to possess more money
        than the caster, it is usual for him on putting his stake in the ring to cry
        "ware caster". The caster then declares, at all under such or such a
        sum, ten, twenty, or fifty pounds, for instance, or else to place against
        the stakes of certain setters the corresponding sums and cry "ware

cover'd only"' (*Monthly Mirror*, January 1807, cited by Hoy, ed., *City Madam*); caster, the one throwing the dice

72   *they* those who have

80   *contemn'd* scorned, i.e. Luke treated Frugal's wealth as something of little value

81   *the case is alter'd* title of a comedy by Ben Jonson (*c.* 1597-8) involving mistaken identities and fluctuating fortunes

83   *discover* uncover, reveal

86   *this* i.e. Shave'em

88   *ka me, ka thee* see above, 2.1.127n

92   *bugbear* imaginary fear

98   *blue gown* worn by prostitutes in houses of correction such as Bridewell

101   *beating hemp* occupation of inmates of Bridewell during its government by Sir Thomas Middleton (1613-1631)

112-3   *suffer/Like a Roman* show courage in the face of adversity

122   *valiant Macedon* Alexander the Great

128   *Genoese* from Genoa, then a rich and important port on the north-west Italian coast

4.3

4   *varlet* knave

5   *millstones* 'to weep millstones': proverbial, not to weep at all (Brewer, *Dictionary of Phrase and Fable*)

13   *piece* coin

15   *other Counter* there were two Counters in London, one at Wood Street, the other at the Poultry (see above, 1.1.35n)

21   *the Fleet* one of the London prisons
       drab frequent prostitutes

25   *bandogs* dogs chained up, either owing to their ferocity, or to guard a house

33   *build upon't* depend upon it

41   *orisons* prayers

44   gratis for free

45   *like ... ears* adders were traditionally said to be deaf

46	*tongues of angels* ironic reference to Corinthians 13.1
50	*farthing* small denomination coin worth a quarter of one old pence
59	*basket* the sheriff's basket, see above 1.1.114n
61	*Jew* employing the stereotype of Jews as avaricious money-lenders
67	*entreats* entreaties, supplications
	imprecations curses (*OED* 1), prayers or petitions (*OED* 2)

4.4

9	*turn'd philosophers* become unworldly and unconcerned with possessions
15	*gallipots* small earthenware glazed pot
19	*bound ... circle* as if they were bewitched (cf. 4.4.23)
26	*buffin* 'coarse cloth in use for the gowns of the middle classes in the time of Elizabeth [I]' (*OED* 1)
27	*show all* go naked
28	*Iwis* certainly
	French hood 'headdress, worn by women in the sixteenth and seventeenth centuries, having the front band depressed over the forehead and raised in folds or loops over the temples' (*OED* 1b)
36	*chandler's* candle maker's
39	*Pimlico* 'place of resort (perhaps from the name of its proprietor) at Hogsdon (now Hoxton), a suburb of London, formerly celebrated for its ale, cakes, etc.' (*OED* 1)
	Islington suburb north of London (not far from Hoxton)
	Save you God save you
46	*bravery* finery
76	*miniver* fur used for lining and trimming ceremonial dress
81	*patrician* member of ruling class in classical Rome; in this case, one of the 'better' citizens of London, from whom aldermen and Lord Mayors would be chosen
	plebeian commoner in classical Rome; in this case, one of the 'lower' citizens of London
84	*auditory* audience
101	*fast ... prenticeship* fast for seven years, the standard term for which an apprentice was bound to his master

106	*carcanets* ornamental collars or necklaces
108	*Hungerland bands* possibly meaning of Hungarian style (the only reference to 'Hungerland' in the *OED* is this line in *The City Madam*)
	quellio *ruffs* Spanish ruffs (from *cuello*, Spanish for collar)
114	*in plate* on silver
123	*since ... more* i.e. princesses have no more conspicuous wealth lavished upon them during their lying-in than Lady Frugal
124	*arras* rich tapestry with scenes and figures woven in colour
125	*waiters* attendants
127	*Tyrian dye* purple dye originally made at Tyre from crushed molluscs
129	*Pompey's Julia* daughter of Julius Caesar and wife of the Roman general Pompey, one time ally of Caesar, later his rival
144	*impression* printed copy
148	*observer* 'one who observers omens' (*OED* 3b); another sense, of 'an obsequious follower' (*OED* 2) is also relevant, although Stargaze himself would not intend this second meaning to be understood
155	*contending* arguing

5.1

7	*close* secret
13.5	SD] Musicians ... arras musicians come down from the gallery to stand behind the arras (tapestry screen) hung up during 4.4; the 'song at [the] arras' presumably refers to the music, demanded by Luke (5.3.36) that accompanies the story of Orpheus in the Underworld
16	*hazard* expose himself to risk
30	*deep* powerful
32	*stripes* lashes
34	*against* for
40	*oblation* offering, sacrifice
	Hecate ancient Greek goddess, associated with the moon, the Underworld, witchcraft and magical rites
54	*honest* faithful to her husband
59	*composition* 'settling of a debt, liability, or claim, by some mutual arrangement' (*OED* 12)

| 68 | *contain* play on two meanings of *contain*: Frugal means that Luke's house will not have the promised Indian gold, because it does not exist (*OED* 1a); Luke understands that his house will not have sufficient capacity for the promised gold because it will be so abundant (*OED* 1b) |

68   *contain* play on two meanings of *contain*: Frugal means that Luke's house will not have the promised Indian gold, because it does not exist (*OED* 1a); Luke understands that his house will not have sufficient capacity for the promised gold because it will be so abundant (*OED* 1b)
75   *moving* affecting, eloquent
78   *reprehension* rebuke
100   *competence* sufficient means to live comfortably (see above, 4.1.99n)
129   *fat* vat
147   *genius* appetite, natural inclination

5.2

2   *cozen'd* deceived
6   *put on* put your hats on (taken off as a sign of respect)
        with … favour referring to Lord Lacy's request for them to put on their hats
7   *your … manner* again, referring to Lord Lacy's request for them to restore their hats
18   *trust* credit
21   *peremptory* decisive, blunt
41   *convince* convict
47   *run out* spent
50   *Partridge Alley* area near Lincoln's Inn frequented by prostitutes
51   *Lambeth Marsh* low-lying area south of the Thames between Lambeth and Blackfriars, notorious as a haunt of criminals and prostitutes
64   *in my danger* in my debt
70   *aquafortis* nitric acid, a powerful corrosive
72   *privileg'd* immune
75   *extent* writ seizing lands in satisfaction of debt
        lowns men of low birth (variant of loon)
79   *for* with

5.3

2   *pictures* Frugal here refers to images of Lacy and Plenty, which are
         revealed later in the scene (5.3.78) and later come to life. One possible
         way of staging this is to hang empty frames, with Lacy and Plenty
         filling the frame and serving as their own 'pictures'

10   *Dutch* reference to the stereotype of the Germans (then known as the
         Dutch) as heavy drinkers (see above 2.1.15n)

12   *cates* delicacies

17   *Jove's nectar* Jove: another name for Jupiter, king of the gods; nectar,
         the drink of the gods

19-21   *vows ... above* indication of a Catholic belief in the cult of the saints

26-27   *number/ ... beads* reference to the Catholic practice of reciting the
         Rosary (a set of fifteen prayers), using a string of beads (a rosary) to
         assist the memory; the worshipper counts off a bead with each prayer

38   *Orpheus* legendary musician from ancient Greece whose music was
         said to charm wild beasts

40   *Charon* figure from classical mythology who rowed the dead across
         the River Styx to the Underworld

41   *Eurydice* Orpheus' wife, lost to him after she died from a snake-bite

42.5   SD] the story of Orpheus in the Underworld after the death of his
         wife Eurydice, Orpheus descended to the Underworld to try to
         recover her; with the power of his music he charmed Cerberus to
         sleep, induced Charon to ferry him across the Styx and persuaded
         Hades, god of the Underworld, and his wife, Persephone, to free
         Eurydice, which they did on condition that she walk before him and
         not look back until they had left the Underworld; before they reached
         the end of the journey out of the Underworld, however, Eurydice
         looked back and was lost to Orpheus once again

43   SD] PLENTY ... behind Plenty and Lacy are ready behind their
         portraits for their entrance at 5.3.108

60   *blue gown* see above, 4.2.98n

65   *flaggy* drooping (referring to the wings of the south wind)

70-1   *terriers/foxes* hunting metaphor

78   *statues* 'loosely used for image' (*OED* 1b)

79   *things indifferent* things to which Luke is indifferent or neutral

104   *superficies* outer surface

107   *perfect* complete

107   SD] Sir Maurice … *descend* the device – where the images of wronged spouses, or future spouses, are brought back to life and reconciled with their errant and repentant partners – is reminiscent of the end of Shakespeare's *The Winter's Tale*, where the statue of Hermione is revived and she is reunited with her husband, Leontes. Where the forces that resurrect Hermione remain mysterious, however, the restitution of Lacy and Plenty is quite obviously a trick

130   *gorgon* mythical monster that turned people into stone if they looked at her

142   *desert* wild, uninhabited region (not necessarily lacking in water or vegetation)

Synopsis

Sir John Frugal is a successful merchant and respected London citizen. The extravagance of his wife and daughters, however, has transformed his previously 'frugal' household into a site of conspicuous, courtly consumption, unbefitting a citizen's family, however rich. Encouraged by the predictions of her astrologer, Stargaze, Lady Frugal encourages a desire for sovereignty in her daughters that deters their suitors, Sir Maurice Lacy and Master Plenty, who had hoped to benefit financially from marriage to Frugal's daughters.

Frugal has also rescued his profligate brother, Luke, from poverty and debtor's prison and has given him refuge within his household, where – ostensibly a reformed and humbled character – he is humiliated and abused by Lady Frugal and her daughters. Despite his veneer of virtue (intervening on behalf of Hoist, Penury and Fortune, his brother's debtors), Luke encourages Young Tradewell and Young Goldwire, Frugal's apprentices, to embezzle money from their master, which they spend on gambling and prostitutes.

Sceptical of Luke's reformation, and wanting to prove his suspicions to Lord Lacy, Frugal resigns control of his wealth and household to his brother and pretends to retire to a monastery, returning (with Lord Lacy's help) accompanied by his daughters' disgruntled suitors disguised as 'Indians' from Virginia to observe Luke's behaviour. Frugal's disquiet about his brother is justified, as Luke – inflamed with avarice – plays the household tyrant. He betrays the apprentices he led astray and engineers their arrest, along with the pimps, gamblers and prostitutes they frequented; he recalls the debts of Hoist, Penury and Fortune without remittance in order to seize the collateral left as security; he strips Lady Frugal and her daughters of their finery, while he goes richly dressed; and he threatens to seize Lord Lacy's manor, pawned to Frugal.

The disguised Frugal tempts Luke to sell Lady Frugal and her daughters to the Indians for human sacrifice, temptation to which Luke succumbs. Frugal then stages a feast and a series of pageants for his brother's birthday, the first depicting the story of Orpheus, placating the hell-dog Cerberus with his music (which leaves the 'beastly', diabolic Luke unmoved). In the second, Luke's victims – Young and Old Goldwire, Young and Old Tradewell, Fortune, Hoist, Penury, Shave'em, Secret, Ding'em, Stargaze and Millicent – appeal for mercy, again without effect. In the final pageant, Lacy and Plenty appear as portraits. As these 'portraits' come alive, Frugal reveals his true identity, and Luke realises he has been tricked. Luke's victims express their repentance and are forgiven; Lacy receives Anne as his wife; Plenty, Mary. Frugal banishes Luke from his household, suggesting he emigrate to Virginia. However, Lady Frugal makes a plea for mercy on Luke's behalf, since his cruelty aided her own reformation and that of her daughters. Luke's final judgement is consequently postponed and the play ends on a moral note, as Frugal instructs his wife and daughters to serve as an example to citizens' wives that they act and dress according to their station, rather than ape court fashions and manners.

TEXTUAL NOTES

This text of *The City Madam* is based on a copy of the 1658 quarto (Q) in the British Library (C.123.d.9), with the prefatory letter (removed from C.123.d.9) copied from BL Ashley 1127. Where this edition departs from the copy-text, it has been checked against the editions of Robert Dodsley (*A Select Collection of Old Plays*, vol. 8, 1744), John Monck Mason (*The Dramatick Works of Philip Massinger*, vol. 4, 1779), W. Gifford (*The Plays of Philip Massinger*, vol. 4, 1805) and Cyrus Hoy (*The City Madam*, 1964). The following notes record all verbal emendations of the text, significant departures in speech prefixes (SPs), and anticipatory stage directions (SDs) that have been omitted or moved substantially. Minor changes to the positioning of SDs are not included. SDs of editorial origin are enclosed in square brackets, but without attribution. The division of acts and scenes follows the 1658 quarto. Readings originating in this edition are designated *this edn*.

Where the participial final *–ed* should be pronounced as a separate syllable, it is printed as *–ed*; where it is not a separate syllable, it is elided to *-'d* (except after *i* or *u*, e.g. *cried*, *sued*). Where the verse lining of the quarto is open to question (in thirteen places), it has been adjusted to fit Massinger's characteristic 'overstuffed' lines of eleven or, occasionally, twelve syllables.

SDs and SPs take the number of the line in which they appear. A decimal point is used for numbering lines within SDs (e.g. 59.5).

Within the quarto, there is some confusion about names: despite being named 'Sir John Frugal' in the text (1.1.32), this character appears as Sir John Rich in the *dramatis personae*, where 'Lady Frugal' also appears as 'Lady Rich'; Lord Lacy's son – called Sir Maurice within the text (1.2.77, 1.2.89) – is named Sir John Lacy in the *dramatis personae*. Following Gifford and Dodsley, these characters have been called, respectively, Sir John Frugal, Lady Frugal and Sir Maurice Lacy.

Dramatis Personae

4   Lady Frugal] *Gifford;* Lady Rich Q
10   Sir Maurice Lacy] *Dodsley;* Sir John Lacie Q
13   Sir John Frugal] *Gifford;* Sir John Rich Q

1.2

60   statute] *Dodsley;* statue *Q*
61   an'] *this edn;* and *Q*
103   SD] *to* [LUKE] *this edn; To him Q*
143-7   marginal SD] *A table, count book, Standish, chair and stools set out Q;*
        moved to beginning of 1.3 *this edn*

1.3

91   reason] *Dodsley;* reasons *Q*
108   And they] *this edn*

2.1

120   instruct] *Mason;* intrust *Q*

2.2

10   marginal SD] *A chair set out Q;* moved to beginning of 2.2 *this edn*
49   SP] *Lacy, Dodsley;* Lady, *Q*
84-5   declare rule, pre-eminence and] *Gifford;* declare preheminence, rule,
        preheminence and *Q*
209   SD] *Both speak weeping Q*

2.3

39   be wi'] *Gifford;* bowy *Q*

3.2

139   their] *Mason;* her *Q*
172   And I am] *Dodsley;* And am *Q*

3.3

30   Fix'd] *Mason;* Fix Q

4.1.

12   an'] *this edn;* and Q

4.2

113   Roman] *Gifford;* Boman Q

5.1

80   ends] Q
95-8   marginal SD] *The Banquet ready. One chair, and Wine.* Q

5.2

69-70   marginal SD] *Plenty ready to speak within* Q; moved to beginning of 5.3
          this edn

5.3

8   marginal SD] *A table and rich banquet* Q
22   By thriving] *Dodsley;* By the thriving Q
45   fiends] *Dodsley;* friends Q
59.5   SD] *directed Dodsley; erected* Q
79   indifferent] *Dodsley;* different Q
107   SD] *Enter Lacie and Plenty* Q
151   instruct] *Dodsley;* mistrust Q

THE
City-Madam,
A
COMEDIE.

Actus primus, Scena prima.

Enter Goldwire, and Tradewell.

Goldwire.
Tradewell.

 He Ship is safe in the Pool then ?
And makes good,
In her rich fraught, the name shee
bears, the *Speedwell* :
My Master will find it, for on my
certain knowledg
For every hundred that hee ven:u-
red in her
She hath return'd him five.

Goldwire. And it comes timely,
For besides a paiment on the nail for a Mannor
I ate purchas'd by my Master, his young daughters
Are ripe for marriage.

B

Facsimile of *The City Madam* (London, 1658), fol. B1.
Reproduced by permission of the British Library (C.123.d.9)